edexcel
advancing learning, changing lives

Edexcel AS History Unit 1
Ideology, Conflict and Retreat: The USA in Asia 1950–1973

Geoff Stewart
Series editors: Derrick Murphy and Angela Leonard

STUDENT BOOK

A PEARSON COMPANY

Contents

Introduction

Welcome to History at AS level. History is a fascinating subject, concerned with the world as it was and how it became the world we know now. By studying History, you will encounter new people, new places, new societies and cultures – even though they are all in the past! If you have an enquiring mind and an interest in the world around you then History is the subject for you.

How to make the most of the course

- Practise your skills. History is not just about learning information or about telling the story of what happened in the past. You need to be able to understand and explain why things turned out the way they did and about how much they changed. The skills builder sections in this book will help you do this.

- Prepare for debate and discussion! Historians do not always agree about why events or developments in the past happened, or about their importance – so don't be afraid to debate with your teacher and other students. But remember that you must give evidence to support any point you make.

- Use the course book. This book has been designed to help you build up the skills, knowledge and understanding to help you do well in your exam – so use it! See the 'How this book will help you' section overleaf for details.

- Read around the subject. The more you learn about a period of history, the more interesting it becomes. Further reading on your chosen topics will broaden your understanding of the period, give you better insights into causation and change, and make the course much more rewarding.

What you will learn

Unit 1 focuses on historical themes in breadth. This means that you need to be able to understand and explain why things changed over a fairly long period. In Option D6 you will learn about how and why the United States became so involved in dramatic political and military events in Asia between 1950 and 1973. You will study the conflict in Korea between 1950 and 1953, into which the USA poured men and money. You will find out about how successive presidents were drawn into a conflict in Vietnam and South East Asia and how they tried to establish a non-Communist state in South Vietnam. You will study the different approaches adopted to try to counter the attempts of the North Vietnamese to infiltrate South Vietnam and re-unify the country under Communist leadership. The growing doubts in the USA about the government's foreign policies and the rise of the protest movements will be examined, as will the reasons for US withdrawal from Vietnam and the means adopted to pull out.

How you will be assessed

For Unit 1 you will take a written exam. You will write two essays: one on each topic you have studied (i.e. one on the USA in Asia and one on your other chosen topic). For each topic you will have a choice of two questions. You will have 1 hour and 20 minutes in total, or 40 minutes for each essay.

How this book will help you

- Clearly written text gives you the historical information you need for this topic in the right amount of depth.

- 'Take note' boxes indicate when you should make notes of your own. These notes will help you with the activities and can also form the basis of your revision, so it's worth keeping up to date with these as you go along.

- Activities help you understand the content and build up your historical skills.

- Skills builder sections help you develop the essential skills you need to do well in your exam.

- Examzone tells you what you need to know to prepare for the exam, including:

— what to expect on the day

— how to revise

— what the assessment objectives mean and how you can meet them

— what the different levels mean and how you can gain a high mark

— example essays with examiner commentaries to help you understand what the examiners are looking for and how to use your information.

Chapter 1   Introduction: power and ideas

Key questions

- What was the basis and extent of the power of the USA in Asia?
- How far was there a conflict about ideas and ideology in Asia?
- Who shaped US policy and why?

The Second World War ended in 1945. Many of the 60 million who died in the war died in Asia, where the war had been fought with a particular savagery. Many in Europe think that the Second World War began in 1939 when Germany attacked Poland. In Asia it began in 1937, when Japan attacked the China of **Chiang Kai-shek (Jiang Jieshi)**. The ultimate loser in Asia was to be Japan, its homeland devastated by bombing and finally forced into a humiliating capitulation involving the hostile occupation of Japan for the first time in that nation's history. Japan had tried to become an Asian superpower, creating a vast empire. The failure was total. The undisputed winner of the Second World War was the United States of America, who in 1945 seemed to dominate East Asia as Japan had tried but failed to do. America's ally in 1945 had been Soviet Russia. Yet five years later the United States was to be involved in another war with a client of the Soviet Union, North Korea.

Timeline

1945	**April:** Truman takes over as US president on the death of Roosevelt **6 August:** Atom bomb dropped on Hiroshima, Japan **2 September:** Japan formally surrenders; US occupies Japan
1946	Civil war in China between the Communists and the Nationalists Republicans gain control of US Congress
1947	Truman announces aid for Greece and the Truman Doctrine National Security Act passed
1948	**June:** Berlin Blockade begins **November:** President Truman narrowly re-elected
1949	**May:** USSR ends the Berlin Blockade **September:** USSR tests first atom bomb **October:** Mao Zedong proclaims the People's Republic of China
1950	**January:** US State Department official Alger Hiss accused of being a Soviet spy and found guilty of perjury **February:** Soviet–Chinese Treaty of Friendship, Alliance and Mutual Assistance signed **April:** NSC 68 produced **June:** North Korea invades South Korea

Power and states in East Asia, 1945–1950

The surrender and occupation of Japan

In August and September 1945, three events seemed to confirm US dominance in the Western Pacific and East Asia. On the morning of 6 August,

Chiang Kai-shek (Jiang Jieshi)

(1887–1975)
Ruler of Nationalist China since 1928. He succeeded in unifying China after devastating wars between different generals but never completely eliminated the Communists in all their base areas. The Japanese assault of 1937 led to the loss of much of China and his retreat to Chungking far up the Yangtze River.

Take note

As you read through this section, consider why the USA was the dominant power in East Asia in 1945. Make a list of the different factors. How far was this dominance a result of temporary circumstances?

US power: devastation in Hiroshima following detonation of the atom bomb, August 1945

Glossary:
Proconsul

A governor of an ancient Roman province.

Glossary:
GNP (Gross National Product)

A measure of the total value of goods and services produced in a country and its overseas earnings. Divided by the number of people, GNP will give an approximate indication of standard of living. It is a useful way of comparing the relative economic importance of countries.

Mao Zedong

(1893–1976)

Chairman of the Chinese Communist Party, which he led since the late 1930s. He became the most important member of the government of the People's Republic of China (PRC) when the Communists won the Civil War in October 1949.

three B-29 long-range bombers reached the Japanese city of Hiroshima. At 8.15 am one of them, the *Enola Gay*, released an atomic bomb from its bomb doors. Nearly 100,000 people were vaporised or incinerated. Thousands more died subsequently of radiation. On 9 August, another plane left the US base at Tinian for Nagasaki. When it dropped an atom bomb on Nagasaki on 9 August, 35,000 people died instantly.

The USA was the sole master of this new awe-inspiring weapon. The Japanese government did as the US government hoped and decided not to continue the fight. On 2 September, on board the battleship USS *Missouri* in Tokyo Bay, General Douglas MacArthur took the formal surrender and became the new ruler of Japan, which had been the greatest power in the region. MacArthur embodied the strength and assertion of the victorious United States, and like some Roman **proconsul** of old, set about governing and transforming this latest 'province' of imperial America.

American dominance in Asia

In fact no other state in the region could come close to equalling the power and might of the USA. The USSR joined the conflict against Japan in the closing days of the war and occupied Manchuria and North Korea, but the Soviet Union was shattered by her exertions in the brutal struggle against Germany. Much of western Russia was devastated and her war effort had become heavily dependent on loans from the USA. The USSR's total **GNP** in 1945 was only a quarter of that of the USA. Vast as the Soviet Army was, it had nothing comparable to the strategic bomber force of the USA or its enormous navy. Nor had the USSR developed the atomic bomb, as yet.

China, the most populous state in the region, was also devastated by its eight long years of struggle against Japan and the corrupt regime of Chiang Kai-shek (Jiang Jieshi), and was heavily dependent on US support. Its army had US instructors attached and in many respects Nationalist China was almost an American satellite. Only the Communists in the north west of China under **Mao Zedong** were independent, but the future seemed to belong to Chiang not Mao. Both Russia and the USA certainly thought so in 1945.

Two other great historic powers of Asia were ghostly shadows of their former imperial might. France was trying to recover from the trauma of defeat and occupation, and faced an uphill struggle to re-impose colonial rule on parts of **Indo-China**: Vietnam, Laos and Cambodia. Britain was, with Russia, the greatest Asiatic power before the war. Britain possessed a vast Indian Empire, Burma and Malaya, and exercised control over much of the trade of southern China. Now, in 1945, she was an exhausted, bankrupt nation, desperate to make ends meet and going, begging bowl in hand, to the USA. Within two years, India, the jewel in the crown of the British Empire, would be abandoned and the bulk of the mighty British navy scrapped. There was, in short, a power vacuum in Asia and into this vacuum stepped '**Uncle Sam**'.

In 1945, US world power was extraordinary. In contrast to the bleak European continent with its rubbled cities and crippled infrastructure, North American cities had remained untouched by bombs and fighting. War had in fact transformed Depression America. Production had leapt as had living standards. The physical output of goods grew by more than 50 per cent, and GNP rose from $88 billion in 1939 to $135 billion in 1945 at 1939 prices ($220 billion in current prices). The US had two-thirds of the world's gold reserves, half the world's shipping and turned out more than half of the world's manufactured goods. War had been good to America. Its armed forces were equally impressive: there were 69 well-equipped divisions in Europe and a further 26 in the Pacific. They commanded the world's oceans with 1200 major warships, and more than 2000 heavy bombers and a further 1000 long-range B29s gave the capacity to punch and destroy any enemy. The siting of the new United Nations in New York was testament to US dominance of the globe at the end of the Second World War.

The shifting balance of power

Yet, five years later, in 1950, America's position of almost unchallenged supremacy seemed to have been undermined, particularly in Asia. The USA was still overwhelmingly the richest nation on Earth and her GNP had continued to grow. (The USSR, despite a measure of economic recovery by 1950, still trailed with a GNP of a mere third of that of the USA.) Despite this, a series of developments appeared to have weakened the United States' global predominance.

Most serious and unexpected was the defeat of the US-backed regime in China under Chiang Kai-shek (Jiang Jieshi). Despite the aid of $2 billion to Jiang, the world's most populous nation had passed under the control of the Communists, led by Mao Zedong. In his high-pitched Hunanese-accented Chinese, Chairman Mao had proclaimed the People's Republic of China in Tiananmen Square on 1 October 1949. At the end of the year, Mao had gone to Moscow and early in 1950 signed an alliance with the Soviet Union. The defeated Nationalists had fled to the island of Taiwan (Formosa) and there prepared to repel the expected invasion from the victorious Communists. The USA was deeply disillusioned with Jiang's regime and did not appear to be inclined to defend it in its island refuge.

Indo-China
Area of South East Asia between China and India and composed of six countries: Myanmar (Burma), Thailand (Siam), Laos, Cambodia, Vietnam and Malaya.

Uncle Sam
Popular expression for the USA, represented in cartoons as a tall, wiry but aging man, clad in the Stars and Stripes.

Take note
As you read through this section, identify the different ways in which US power and dominance in Asia had declined between 1945 and 1950.
What was the most serious cause of the decline?

Joseph Stalin

(1879–1953)

The effective and largely unchallenged ruler of the USSR from 1929 until his death in 1953. Between 1924 and 1929, he outmanoeuvred all potential rivals to succeed Lenin, and later had them murdered or executed. He transformed the USSR by policies of rapid industrialisation and collectivisation and emerged from the Second World War as one of the most feared and admired men on Earth.

Lavrenty Beria

(1899–1953)

Stalin's henchman from the same area of the Soviet empire, Georgia, and equally feared as the head of the secret police from 1938 to 1953.

Harry S. Truman

(1884–1972)

President of the USA from 1945 to 1953 in succession to Roosevelt, who had died in office. He had never expected to be president and always felt under-qualified, never having been to university or risen above the rank of captain when serving in the army. To many of his critics he remained a small-town politician promoted beyond his abilities, but most historians today consider him an able and impressive president.

In Indo-China, France was struggling to resist Communist/Nationalist forces under the leadership of Ho Chi Minh. Even in Japan, US power was under attack, with Communist-inspired demonstrations challenging American control.

Superpower rivalry: relations between the USA and the USSR

At the other side of the Asian landmass, Soviet military power gripped Eastern Europe. The US Army had been rapidly run down after the war and was short of all kinds of equipment. Once peace came, Truman's government cut defence spending savagely: in 1948 the US spent only $10.9 billion compared to Russia's $13.1 billion. Despite an American increase in defence spending to $13.5 billion in 1949, there appeared to be a growing gap in the military balance of power. The USSR had an army of 2.6 million with 30 armoured divisions; the USA's army totalled 640,000 with one armoured division. The excellent MiG-15 jet fighter had come into service in 1949–50, and the USSR was building up a strategic bomber force, producing 7000 planes of all types a year to the 1200 produced in the United States. A month before Mao proclaimed the People's Republic of China in October 1949, US aircraft picked up signs of a vast radioactive cloud off the Russian peninsula of Kamchatka. The USA was no longer the world's only nuclear power. At the end of August 1949, **Stalin** had got the news he had been waiting for from his sinister secret police chief, **Beria**: Russia had successfully tested a nuclear bomb.

It was in the context of a perception of growing weakness that a secret report on America's military strength was produced in April 1950. It was to be known as NSC 68 (being paper No. 68 of the National Security Council). Its author was Paul Nitze, acting under the direction of Secretary of State **Dean Acheson**. It attempted to answer the question of what the USA should be spending on defence to contain the USSR. It arrived at the shocking conclusion that defence spending should be increased to somewhere in the order of $35 to $50 billion annually. President **Truman** was cautious and refused to publicise the report. The rapid expansion ran counter to his whole policy hitherto. As his biographer, David McCullough, concludes: 'Whether he would have attempted anything like the build-up called for in NSC 68 had events not taken the calamitous turn they did in late June, will never be

Dean Acheson

(1893–1971)

Dean Acheson, Truman's secretary of state, was a complete contrast to the president, coming from the east-coast elite, attending one of the top private schools and then both Yale and Harvard Law School – two of the most prestigious universities in the US. During the years he served under Truman, Acheson was instrumental in consolidating the NATO alliance, the Truman Doctrine (see p. 11) and the Marshall Plan. He helped to develop America's post-war policy towards Germany, the Soviet Union and the People's Republic of China, and was closely involved in diplomatic negotiations during the Korean Conflict. After his retirement from politics, he returned to his law practice but served as adviser to presidents Kennedy, Johnson and Nixon.

known. But it seems unlikely.' It was events in Korea in June 1950 that would therefore see NSC 68 become reality (see Chapter 2, page 21).

Ideology and the Cold War context

By 1950, the **war-time alliance** had seriously fragmented and the world's two greatest powers now faced one another in a game of diplomatic and military confrontation. The development of this confrontation was complex and its roots much disputed by historians. At one level it was a good old-fashioned example of great-power rivalry. Throughout the nineteenth century, Tsarist Russia and Britain had played what had been termed the 'great game' for the domination of Asia. In one sense the USA had inherited Britain's role. This viewpoint was well expressed in a secret OSS (US special operations and the ancestor of the CIA) report presented to President Roosevelt, just before his death in April 1945.

> *Russia will emerge from the present conflict as by far the strongest nation in Europe and Asia – strong enough, if the United States should stand aside, to dominate Europe and at the same time to establish her hegemony over Asia. Russia's natural resources and manpower are so great that within a few years she can be much more powerful than either Germany or Japan has ever been. In the easily foreseeable future Russia may well outrank even the United States in military potential.*

War-time alliance
This refers to the 'Big Three' opponents of Germany and Japan, namely Britain, the USSR and the USA.

Take note
Draw a diagram to illustrate what gives a country power and influence.

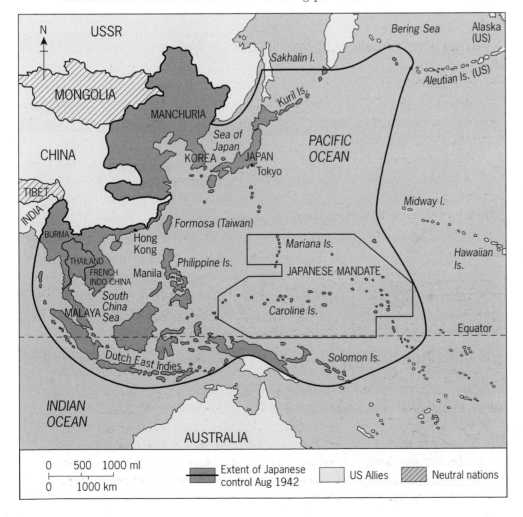

East Asia in 1942

To the Western powers, Russia looked more powerful than it really was. Stalin was well aware of Russia's historical backwardness and her vulnerability to a series of invaders from the west, the latest of whom had been Nazi Germany. Swedes, Poles, French and Germans had marched east to seize parts of 'Mother Russia' at various times. Stalin was determined to prevent a repeat invasion, and much that appeared aggressive to the West arose from a partially justified paranoia on Stalin's part. Russia was vulnerable, and pushing westwards into Eastern Europe could safeguard the motherland. After the Second World War ended, the border of Soviet Russia was pushed westward and Soviet troops installed communist governments in all the nominally independent countries of Eastern Europe. To the West, the expansion of Soviet control in Europe was perceived as a threat, and similar aggression was expected on the part of the Soviet Union in Asia.

The clash of ideas

However, there was an added ingredient – ideological confrontation – and this made the clash more bitter and more dangerous. Even in Britain's rivalry with Tsarist Russia there had been an element of ideology. Britain saw herself as a liberal power standing for the most advanced values of the age; in contrast, Tsarist Russia was perceived as a bastion of reactionary stupidity and despotism.

The USSR: ideology

In 1950 the USSR was the champion of **'Marxist Leninism'** and espoused world revolution. The Soviet regime openly proclaimed its belief that there could be no long-term peace between capitalism and communism, and that communism would eventually triumph throughout the world. The USSR now saw itself as the face of progress and the USA as the bastion of capitalist selfishness. The Great Depression of 1929–1933 and then the war against Nazi Germany had given Stalin's Russia a credibility it did not deserve as the hope of mankind. Many in the West among the intelligentsia believed in the Soviet Union as the solution to the world's ills – a utopia in the making. George Bernard Shaw, the eminent British playwright, was famously filmed on a Soviet collective farm in 1932 proclaiming the superiority of the Soviet system. There was no mention of the horrific famine in southern Russia in that year, induced by Stalin's policies, which put any suffering in the West brought about by the Great Depression in the shade. Indeed, there was an ample supply of willing Soviet agents in the West prepared to betray their countries for the communist dream. In Britain, members of the British elite, such as Guy Burgess, Kim Philby and Anthony Blunt, supplied the USSR with classified information. In the USA, Alger Hiss in the State Department supplied state secrets to the Soviet Union, and Julius and Ethel Rosenberg were part of a spy network feeding atomic secrets to Russia. There was an idealism about communism among many in the West, and the realities of Soviet Russia were often overlooked or forgotten as a result of distaste for the failings of Western societies. These failings, unemployment, poverty etc. loomed large but were undoubtedly lesser failings than the atrocities meted out by Lenin and Stalin.

Take note

What made many in the West sympathise with communism and the USSR?

Glossary:
Marxist Leninism

The official belief system of the USSR based on the ideas of Karl Marx (1818–1883) as interpreted by Lenin. It was a godless religion, claiming to be based on science.

While celebrated as the champion of communism by Western idealists, Soviet Russia was, for those living there, a brutal, oppressive regime. The world of Ivan the Terrible, the monstrous ruler of sixteenth-century Russia, had been recreated and he remained one of Stalin's heroes. Hundreds of thousands had died in the purges of 1936–1938 and many more suffered a living death in the freezing gulags (prison camps) of Siberia and the Arctic north. Arbitrary arrest, torture and a total disregard for the rule of law marked the Soviet system. This, it must be said, had probably little to do with communism but merely reflected the primitive level of development of Russia in terms of human rights. The Bolshevik Revolution of 1917, far from advancing Russia, had actually turned the clock back from a moderately authoritarian Tsarist regime to one of incredible brutality. Lenin's new government had murdered more people in the first year of its existence than in the 23 years of Tsar Nicholas II's reign. Stalin surpassed Lenin, and only Hitler among his contemporaries could rival Stalin's capacity for political murder which bordered on genocide.

The USA: attitudes and ideology

In the light of this Soviet track record, it is not surprising that the leaders of the USA felt distaste. Much was wrong with American society, as President Truman was aware. Endemic racism in the southern states had yet to be moderated by the civil rights movement. There were great inequalities of wealth, yet there was freedom and the rule of law, and this is what Truman and his associates saw themselves as defending against the Soviet regime. As early as April 1945, Averell Harriman, Roosevelt's ambassador to Moscow, had written:

> *The Soviet Union and the minority governments that the Soviets are forcing on the people of Eastern Europe have an entirely different objective. We must clearly recognise that the Soviet program is the establishment of totalitarianism, ending personal liberty and democracy as we know and respect it.*

US President Truman put the conflict simply in his famous speech of 1947, announcing aid for Greece and defining what became known as the **Truman Doctrine**.

> *At the present moment in world history nearly every nation must choose between alternative ways of life. The choice is too often not a free one.*
>
> *One way of life is based upon the will of the majority, and is distinguished by free institutions, representative government, free elections, guarantees of individual liberty, freedom of speech and religion, and freedom from political oppression. The second way of life is based upon the will of the minority forcibly imposed on the majority. It relies upon terror and oppression, a controlled press and radio, fixed elections and the suppression of personal freedoms.*

It is easy to sympathise with Truman, who was utterly sincere in his statement. To him and many like him there was increasingly little to choose between Stalin and the defeated Hitler. Both threatened the world of freedom and choice. Yet as the famous American journalist, Walter Lippmann, wrote

Take note

Why did Truman and many in the West feel that the USSR and communism had to be resisted?

Truman Doctrine

On 12 March 1947 President Truman announced to Congress details of what became known as the Truman Doctrine. He addressed Congress to ask for $400 million in aid for Greece and Turkey, and to request that American military and economic advisers be sent to both countries. Its purpose was to overcome widespread opposition within the United States to direct involvement in Europe and to ensure that neither Greece nor Turkey fell under Soviet control.

Take note

As you read through this section, write down the functions of the US organisations in the chart below:

Organisation	Function	Example of influence
Secretary of State and State Department		
NSC		
CIA		
FBI		
Senate		
House of Representatives		

The US Constitution of 1787

The Constitution had rigidly divided the separate spheres of the US political system into:

- an executive branch headed by the president, elected every four years
- a legislative branch (Congress) composed of the Senate and House of Representatives
- the judicial branch headed by the Supreme Court.

Each was deliberately designed to check the others and ensure good government without abuse of power. This is referred to as the 'separation of the powers'.

at the time about the implications of the Truman Doctrine, 'A vague global policy which sounds like the tocsin [alarm bell] of an ideological crusade, has no limits. It cannot be controlled. Its effects cannot be predicted.' Lippmann was right: much trouble was being stored up for the USA and the world in the name of a crusade for liberty.

The US domestic context – the shaping of policy

The process of political decision making was complex, involving extensive consultation and weighing of evidence, even in the non-democratic states of China and the USSR. Both Mao and Stalin consulted the senior figures in the ruling elite; in the Soviet Union, Stalin had the final say. Neither the Soviet Union nor China had a free press to complicate matters. In addition, public opinion could be largely discounted.

In the United States, the process was far more complicated. Here the press and public opinion were a considerable influence, and the **US Constitution** deliberately shared power among different institutions to guard against the sort of authoritarian abuse that marked the two communist regimes.

The central, but by no means all-powerful, figure of the American system was the president. Five presidents occupied the White House between 1950 and 1973: Truman, Eisenhower, Kennedy, Johnson and Nixon. They were five very different personalities but none could be discounted.

Developments under President Truman

Harry S. Truman was the president in 1950 and, on the surface, the least impressive and imposing of the five. Like the then British prime minister, Clement Attlee, whom Churchill had described as a 'modest little man with much to be modest about', Truman had achieved power unexpectedly in 1945. As vice president he succeeded on the death of the towering figure of Franklin Roosevelt. Truman had little knowledge of foreign policy, had not been to university and always suffered from somewhat shaky spelling. However, he learned quickly, knew how and where to take good advice, and after careful thought was decisive. He impressed contemporaries like Churchill and gained the respect and liking of his staff. Despite most predictions to the contrary, he won the presidential election of 1948 against a strong Republican challenger and then stood down in 1953. It was during his time in the White House that the Cold War was launched and the USA became involved in the crisis in Korea. He tended to have a rather simple black-and-white view of the world and morality. The oppression and apparent aggression of Soviet Russia appalled him, and while wishing to avoid a third world war, he was not prepared to be pushed around. He adopted the policy of 'containment': communism should be accepted in the areas where it had established itself but resisted if it sought to expand. Truman believed that such an intrinsically wicked system would eventually fail if it were contained.

Each president relied heavily on numerous advisers. In theory the most important was the secretary of state, who was responsible for foreign policy.

In Truman's case, theory and reality coincided. Dean Acheson served Truman throughout his second term (1949–1953) and was referred to by the president as his 'top brain man'. Truman, the humble farm boy from Missouri, and Acheson, the always immaculately dressed east-coast lawyer, who had attended Yale and Harvard, were contrasting figures but worked well together. Acheson exuded intellectual and social superiority, which alienated many. Senator Hugh Butler of Nebraska expressed the distaste that many ordinary Americans felt: 'I look at that fellow, I watch his smart-aleck manner and his British clothes and I, want to shout, "Get out! Get out!" You stand for everything that has been wrong in the United States for years.'

Those whom Acheson alienated, Truman could reach out to. Through his more simplistic style, Truman was able to translate the sophisticated ideas of the State Department elite to US citizens.

National Security Act of 1947

The State Department was the traditional shaper and conductor of foreign policy but the National Security Act of 1947 added new institutions. The National Security Council was set up to advise the president in the new context of the Cold War. It had at its disposal a growing army of experts and analysts and produced a series of influential policy statements, such as NSC 68 (see page 8). Another new organisation set up under the National Security Act was the Central Intelligence Agency, or CIA. Many were suspicious of such a body, seeing it as essentially 'un-American' and a threat to traditional libertarian values, but in the context of the growing rivalry with the USSR it gradually grew in numbers and enjoyed an escalating budget, both for intelligence gathering and covert operations. Also highly influential and working for the secretary of defence and the president were the Joint Chiefs of Staff, composed of the respective heads of the armed services. All of these offices formed part of an expanding executive.

However, unlike the political system in the USSR, the US executive could not operate without the co-operation of the legislature. The American president and his advisers had to work with Congress to secure money and new laws if they were necessary.

- The House of Representatives, composed of 435 members and divided between the various states according to their population, was elected every two years. In 1946 the Democrats lost their long-standing majority to the Republicans, increasing Truman's problems. This was particularly true of foreign policy, where a powerful group in the Republican Party pressed the US government to do more to help Chiang Kai-shek (Jiang Jieshi). In general, the more moderate Republicans predominated and they were willing to work with the president on most questions.
- The upper house was the Senate, with two senators from every state elected for six years. It played a major part, both in making laws but also in having to approve the president's choice of ministers in his cabinet. Once again, Truman lost a Democratic majority here in 1946.

Democrats versus Republicans

The Democratic Party had held the presidency since 1933 and usually controlled both houses of Congress. It was the more 'liberal' or left-wing of the two parties. However, although southern Whites were traditionally Democrat, they were anything but liberal or left-wing. The Republicans were the party of big business and western farmers.

McCarthyism

One of the least impressive members of the Senate was to give Truman cause for concern from 1950 onwards, and in the process illustrate the power of public opinion and the press. Senator Joseph McCarthy of Wisconsin had been voted the worst senator by press correspondents serving in Washington. He had few political friends, even within his own Republican Party. In 1950, however, a dinner companion, who was a Catholic priest, suggested that he might raise his profile by launching a campaign against communist infiltration of the government. As one journalist pointed out, Joe McCarthy knew little about communism and could not tell Karl Marx from Groucho Marx (an American comedian and film star). However, McCarthy was not one to let ignorance stand in the way of a good idea, and a month later he made a speech in which he claimed that he knew of 205 communists in the State Department. Over the next few weeks more speeches followed. The numbers changed but not the message. Although no evidence was produced, the public began gradually to take notice and the smears started to have an effect. Some fellow Republicans in the Senate and House of Representatives began to lend support to McCarthy's campaign, and even some Democrats. Joseph Kennedy of Massachusetts and his up-and-coming young congressman son, Jack, were sympathetic – they had a large number of anti-communist **Catholic constituents**. Anti-communist sentiment was intensified and Truman's and Acheson's conduct of foreign policy made more difficult by the furore.

The Red Scare

The roots of the anti-communist hysteria, or the 'Red Scare', were many and varied. There had been serious Soviet penetration of the USA in the 1930s and early 1940s. In 1941, we now know, there had been 221 NKVD (Soviet secret intelligence and police) agents in the USA reporting back to Beria and more GRU (Soviet Army Intelligence) agents reporting back to the Red Army. Stalin knew more about the Manhattan project (the building of the atom bomb) than Truman did as vice president. A well-connected diplomat in the State Department, Alger Hiss, a friend of Acheson, had been supplying the Soviets with diplomatic secrets at the time of the Yalta conference (February 1945). In January 1950, Hiss was found guilty of perjury (lying under oath) and sentenced to five years' imprisonment. Most other Soviet agents had been rounded up between 1945 and 1950 by the FBI, the government organisation responsible for checking inter-state crime and internal threats to US security. Truman's government had tightened up with increased loyalty tests and, some would say, excessive security precautions in 1947–1948. In this sense, the real threat was over by the time McCarthy got into the act. However, the final Hiss verdict, the new awareness that Russia now had a bomb and the fact that China had been 'lost' to Communism, all created a mounting hysteria in 1950s America, which it was difficult to resist. The attacks reached to the highest levels of Truman's administration: Acheson himself was repeatedly attacked as was General Marshall, the secretary of defence and the other great prop to Truman in the conduct of foreign policy. It was in this context that news arrived on 25 June that communist troops from North Korea had invaded South Korea, which was governed by a US-backed regime.

Take note

Identify the factors that created McCarthyism in the early 1950s.

Glossary: Catholic constituents

Many Roman Catholics in the USA had connections with Eastern Europe and deeply resented the Soviet occupation of countries such as Poland and Hungary where the Roman Catholic church was now persecuted.

Activity: The balance of power in Asia

1. Study the map of East Asia in 1942 on page 9 and use the information in this chapter to identify the positions of the following:
   - the USA (and its major base, Pearl Harbor in Hawaii)
   - the USSR
   - Japan
   - China
   - British territory
   - French territory.

2. Where were US troops stationed by the end of 1945?

3. Produce a timeline graph of 1945–1950, marking on it the points where the USA's power suffered a setback.

Taking it further

Try to find out more about the key US figure during this period, Harry S. Truman. There is a short essay on him in a recent book on the twentieth-century American presidents, called *The Presidents* by Stephen Graubard (2004). For those who really enjoy reading there is a magnificent biography by David McCullough, *Truman* (1992).

Chapter 2   The origins of the Korean War

Key questions

- Why was Korea a point of tension by 1950?
- Why did the forces of North Korea attack South Korea in June 1950?
- Why did the USA decide to give such extensive help to South Korea?

The Korean War is often referred to as the 'Forgotten War'. Technically it was not a war at all; the USA officially referred to it as a 'police action'. The United States government never declared war on the power that became its chief opponent – the People's Republic of China. Likewise, China never declared war on the USA. Soviet pilots assisted the North Koreans and Chinese, but officially they were not there. The USA also pretended they were not there. For all the pretence, it was a brutal, bloody conflict fought on an inhospitable spur of Asia and at times it looked as if it would develop into a third world war.

Timeline

1905	Korea falls under Japanese control following the Russo–Japanese war
1910	Korea formally annexed to Japan
1945	**August:** 38th parallel accepted by USA and USSR as a dividing line between North and South Korea **December:** Moscow Accords signed
1947	UN Commission on Korea to oversee elections
1948	**February:** North Korean People's Army established **May:** Elections in South Korea **August:** Republic of South Korea (ROK) established with Syngman Rhee as president **September:** Democratic People's Republic of Korea (DPRK) established, headed by Kim Il Sung **December:** Last Soviet troops leave North Korea
1949	**March:** Kim Il Sung goes to Moscow to ask for military aid; Stalin agrees to send armaments to North Korea **September:** US troops leave South Korea
1950	**January:** Acheson's Press Club speech outlines US defence perimeter **February:** Soviet–Chinese Treaty of Friendship, Alliance and Mutual Assistance signed **April:** Kim Il Sung goes to Moscow to obtain the USSR's approval for the invasion of South Korea **June:** North Korea invades South Korea

Take note

As you read though this section, make notes on the following points:
1. What effects did Korea's three great neighbours have on Korea by 1945?
2. Why was Korea divided in 1945?

The roots of the Korean War

Few members of the general public in either Britain or the United States had ever heard of Korea in June 1950, let alone were able to place it on a map of the world. Certainly, Korea had been of little interest to the governments of either country. It was a mountainous peninsula jutting out from Asia into the Pacific Ocean and lying on roughly the same lines of latitude as Washington DC and Spain. It was not large, being roughly 600 miles from north to south and 150 miles from east to west. It had little to commend it as a place to fight a war. Like Britain, it was surrounded by water (apart from the northern border), but unlike Britain it had no gulf stream to soften the climate. Boiling, muggy summers with temperatures of 38 degrees Celsius were followed by freezing Siberian-style winters. Hills and mountains predominated and the prevailing colour was brown. Everywhere, US and British troops were to comment on the stench of human excrement used to fertilise the fields.

In view of the above qualities, it might be supposed that the Korean people would be left alone. Unfortunately, this small Asian kingdom was right in the middle of three powerful neighbours. To the north and west lay China, traditionally known as the 'elder brother' in Korea. From China had come much of Korea's culture and religion, and powerful Chinese emperors had always claimed a vague over-lordship. Despite ancient connections, the language of Korea was not Chinese but a complex Asiatic one related to Finnish. (Hardly any Americans were able to learn and speak it.) Also to the north lay Russia, and in the late-nineteenth century this vast European/ Asian state began to develop an interest in the area. At the same time, Korea's eastern neighbour, Japan, just over a hundred miles across the sea, was also beginning to develop an interest. In 1895 Japan defeated Imperial China and gained control of Korea; it later deposed the native Yi dynasty in 1905 when Japan also defeated Russia.

For the next forty years the Korean people were the subject of brutal Japanese rule and repeated attempts to wipe out their culture and replace it with a Japanese one. Korean patriots were murdered and exile was the common fate of many. During this period, two of the most important national figures both left their native land but hoped to return to lead an independent state. The elder of the two, Doctor Syngman Rhee, was a Christian and spoke English. He had been sent to the USA in 1905 in the hope he could assist the cause of Korean independence in the talks that brought about peace between Russia and Japan. He failed, but stayed on in the USA developing many powerful contacts and never ceased to press the claims of his people. The other figure was younger, but an equally fervent nationalist. Born Kim Song Ju in 1912, his parents tried to escape Japanese rule and moved into Chinese Manchuria. Here Kim learned Chinese. He joined the Chinese Communist Party and took a new name, Kim Il Sung, by which he is always known. From 1932 to 1940 he led a guerrilla group against the Japanese, but facing defeat and death fled to the Soviet Union where he became a member of the Soviet Army and, by the end of the Second World War, a battalion commander. He became thoroughly indoctrinated with loyalty to his adopted country and filled with deference to its great leader, Comrade Stalin. The defeat of Japan in August 1945 suddenly made possible the fulfilment of both Kim's and Syngman's dreams: an independent Korea.

The division of Korea

Russia had agreed to join in the war against Japan when it appeared that the final struggle might be long and hard. The use of the atomic bomb meant that the USA did not need them in the end, but Soviet troops poured into Manchuria (northern China) and into the Korean Peninsula. As with Germany, it was essential to arrive at a dividing line between the victorious allies. The suddenness of Japan's collapse took the US State Department by

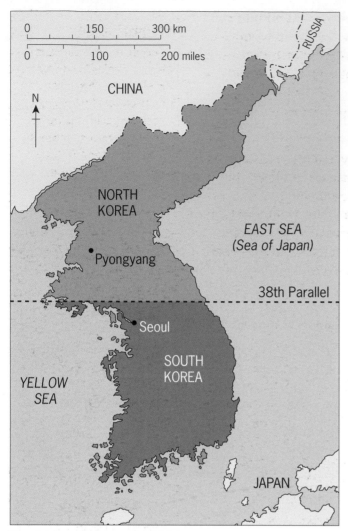

The division of Korea at the 38th parallel

Totalitarian state

Phrase used to describe a country in which the government seeks to control all aspects of the individual's life. George Orwell created an imaginary version of this in his novel *1984* (published in 1949). He modelled his fantasy on the Soviet Russia of Stalin, where all feared the secret police and industry was owned by the state, as was agriculture, which had been collectivised.

surprise – there were no American troops in Korea. At 2 am on the morning of 11 August, the State Department rang Brigadier General Lincoln of the Army Operations Office in Washington and asked for a halt line. Lincoln looked at the map he had available, noticed the 38th parallel and plumped for that. Rather to the surprise of the State Department, the Soviets accepted it. The USA rushed troops to Korea with orders to halt at the 38th parallel. Thus were two Koreas born, and Kim and Rhee were both to have states. Kim Il Sung arrived first, in North Korea in September 1945; Syngman Rhee arrived a month later into the American zone.

The establishment of the North Korean state

The USSR appears to have been better prepared for how it proposed to run its occupied zone. It had the advantage of several thousand native Koreans who had either served with the Chinese Communists or, like Kim, with the Soviet Red Army. It was to the latter that real power was to be entrusted. Kim was welcomed in a public celebration as early as October 1945. Such events were clearly orchestrated by the occupying Soviet forces. In February 1946 an Interim People's Committee was set up under Kim's chairmanship. This was tantamount to the establishment of a trainee North Korean government. Initially co-operation was sought with various leftist elements, including a few Christians. Populist policies were introduced involving the redistribution of land to the peasants. Many of the landowning class had co-operated with the Japanese, and many of these and the junior administrators under Japanese rule now began to flee from the North and enter the US zone. 800,000 were eventually to cross the 38th parallel heading south. Gradually Soviet-influenced Communists were inserted into all the leading positions in the North at the expense of those with Chinese links. Independent liberal leftists were sidelined or arrested, and a police state based on a Soviet-style army and secret police increasingly controlled all aspects of life. Government informants penetrated all parts of society. The press in the North regurgitated the official line. A mini-version of the Soviet **totalitarian state** had been created. Whether this had always been planned or was a response to the Cold War elsewhere is impossible to declare.

In September 1948 an independent government was established in North Korea and the Soviet forces formally withdrew; the withdrawal was completed by December. It left behind, however, a docile **puppet state**. There was a well-staffed Soviet embassy and Soviet mission; a host of Soviet advisers and technicians directed the reviving heavy industry of the North, and exports of strategic materials to Russia were stepped up. As with the Soviet Union, the emphasis was overwhelmingly on heavy industry, not consumer goods. The key institution came to be the NKPA (North Korean People's Army), established in February 1948. It was placed under Soviet-trained commanders like Kim with a plentiful supply of advisers (150 per division) and Soviet equipment. The NKPA enjoyed a privileged position inside North Korea in terms of food and status.

That this new North Korean state was not a democracy is not surprising. There was no democratic tradition in Korea and, at least at this stage in its existence, the corruption that plagued the South was less in evidence in Kim Il Sung's new kingdom. Nevertheless, it was far from a people's paradise. **Collectivisation** was to take back the land from the peasants. An oppressive state replaced the old landlord class, and the degree of tight control exceeded anything that they and their Japanese masters had managed.

South Korea

In the South the US forces appear to have been far less prepared for the administration of Korea. Very few Americans could speak Korean and, initially, the US Army under General Hodge had to rely on Japanese officials, which caused much resentment. Later, native Koreans who had served under the Japanese tended to achieve prominence, although they often suffered from a residual resentment from the rural population as ex-collaborators with the hated occupiers. Rhee emerged in the South as the most effective political leader with a reputation for resistance to Japanese rule. He had strong links to the Chiang Kai-shek (Jiang Jieshi) regime in China and was not well loved by the State Department. Acheson had written of him in 1945:

> *His sympathy toward conservative banking, landlord and merchant classes, his opposition to the **Moscow accords**, his uncompromising attitude towards those who opposed him and his close association with a number of Koreans who advocate the Korean cause solely for personal advantage, alienated many moderate elements and identified him as a right wing extremist.*

Hodge, a much more conservative figure than Acheson, also found Rhee difficult, but it was hard to find a suitable replacement. Acheson had had to admit to Rhee's 'great emotional popularity'.

The USA was increasingly anxious to pull out of Korea. The South was riddled with factional divisions and banditry and was hardly the most promising territory for a fledgling democracy. Reluctantly the US authorities came to accept that Rhee was the best they had, and he and his associated Korean Democratic Party (KDP) assumed power after winning the UN-supervised elections of May 1948. However, many left-wing parties refused to compete and North Korea refused to allow the UN commission in.

The new assembly elected Syngman Rhee president and the Republic of Korea came into existence on the 15 August 1948. An authoritarian and corrupt South faced an oppressive and totalitarian North. Neither accepted

Puppet state

Country which in theory is independent but in reality is controlled by another, more powerful state. In the post-war period, the USSR created puppet communist states in Eastern Europe, such as Bulgaria, Poland and East Germany.

Glossary: Collectivisation

This is a policy whereby enterprises and especially farms come under collective group ownership and ultimately state control. Workers work for the state and not directly for themselves.

Moscow accords, December 1945

This was an agreement signed by the foreign ministers of the USA and USSR in Moscow to establish a Joint Soviet–American Commission to supervise the process leading to Korean independence.

the other as legitimate and both claimed to speak for the whole of Korea. Civil war or permanent partition was inevitable, but neither Kim nor Rhee accepted partition. War would come whenever one of their patrons, the USA or the USSR, accepted it as desirable.

Why did the forces of North Korea attack South Korea in June 1950?

Conflict, in the form of border raids, began in 1949. Both sides showed aggression, and in the sense that the Korean War was a civil war, it began in that year not 1950. Kim begged for help in attacking the South but Stalin refused permission. The Republic of Korea's forces launched small-scale attacks, but the USA refused to supply the hardware necessary to make a real invasion of the North possible. The USA did establish an advisory body to help develop a South Korean Army, but the function as conceived by the USA was primarily defensive. KMAG (Korean Military Advisory Group) was established and was soon known among US troops as 'Kiss My Ass Goodbye', a possible indication of their lack of enthusiasm for their assigned task. Both North and South Korea, in other words, were squaring up to one another in 1949 but did not dare to launch a full-blooded attack. This was to change in 1950, and the change came primarily from the Soviet Union.

Stalin, in 1949, had been a restraining influence on Kim Il Sung, but in 1950 the bonds of restraint were snapped for a variety of reasons. Even in 1949, the Soviet Union was generous with military equipment: 87 T-34 tanks were supplied, as well as various armoured vehicles and self-propelled guns. This was equipment for attack not defence. Military aircraft were also supplied, and most ominous for the South was the return of 50,000 hardened veterans who had served with the People's Liberation Army (PLA) in China's civil war. These were to form the spearhead of the North's attacking forces.

Stalin appears to have accelerated the pace of arming Kim in February 1950. Equipment for a further three divisions was made available. More T-34 tanks, SU-76 self-propelled guns, heavy howitzers and – a clear sign of the aggressive intent – river-crossing gear, were all poured into Ch'ongjin Harbour in April and May. By June there was a formidable aggressive force with 242 tanks and over 200 aircraft on the North side of the 38th parallel.

There is still controversy over what led Stalin to change his mind and give the green light to Kim. What is beyond doubt is that the attack could not have taken place without Stalin's approval and it was only made possible by the massive rearming of the NKPA by the Soviet Union. Most commentators accept that the initiative came from Kim, but Beria's son, in his memoirs, asserts that it was Stalin himself who pressed for the attack. Certainly, he was more confident in the USSR's military position in Asia. He had ended the American nuclear monopoly in 1949 with the successful testing of an atom bomb and the success of Mao's forces in China massively swung the balance against the USA. Mao and Stalin concluded a military pact in February 1950, and it appears that the wily Soviet dictator felt that if the worst came to the

Take note

As you work through pages 20–22, answer the following questions.

1. Why was Kim Il Sung able to attack South Korea with hope of success in June 1950?
2. Why was Stalin feeling more confident regarding Soviet power in Asia in 1950?
3. Why did the USA decide to intervene militarily in the last week of June 1950?

Set your answers out in a table:

	Reasons	Evidence
Kim Il Sung		
Stalin		
USA		

worst and the USA became militarily involved, then Chinese troops could 'pull the chestnuts out of the fire' and save Kim's forces without direct Soviet intervention. This would have the added advantage of permanently dividing China from the USA and making it more dependent on the USSR.

In fact, Stalin appears to have hoped that the USA would not intervene in the coming conflict. US troops had withdrawn from South Korea in 1949 and those in Japan were poorly equipped. It is often argued that Stalin was influenced by a speech made by Dean Acheson on 12 January 1950, when the US secretary of state defined the US Pacific defence perimeter as excluding territory in mainland Asia. However, there is no real evidence from the Soviet Union that this was influential. Probably more important was a secret National Security Committee paper, NSC 48, made available to Stalin by Soviet spies, notably the British liaison officer with the CIA, Kim Philby. This document again tended to imply that South Korea was not a vital US interest.

Stalin gave North Korea the go-ahead and urged its leader to seek Mao's blessing as well. This was duly given, and at 4 am on Sunday 25 June, the North launched a massive attack across the 38th parallel towards the Southern capital of Seoul. Kim Il Sung hoped to finish the conquest of the South in a few weeks.

Why did the USA decide to intervene?

Clearly the USA did not seek conflict in Korea. They had deliberately withheld heavy equipment from the Republic of South Korea (ROK) Army to prevent Rhee launching an attack on the North. The South Korean forces had only 27 light armoured vehicles and no tanks; they possessed 22 aircraft. They had no answer to the T-34 tanks of the In Min Gun (North Korean forces) – their anti-tank rocket launchers fired missiles that bounced harmlessly off the North Korean tanks. In two days, the South Korean capital fell to advancing Communist forces and the ROK Army was in full retreat. On 29–30 June, General MacArthur, the supreme US commander in the region, informed Washington that the Republic of Korea was likely to collapse without extensive US assistance and recommended sending two US divisions from Japan.

Already, the two most important decision makers in the USA had decided that the aggression of the North should be resisted. The attack on South Korea was a flagrant breach of the US–Soviet Agreement of August 1945 and of the UN recognition of the legitimacy of the Republic of Korea. When Acheson had defined the US defence perimeter in January as excluding Korea, he had added that the UN had an obligation to defend sovereign states and implied that the USA would support this. It was as far as he could go at the time. He could not, off his own bat, formally extend the USA's commitments in Asia, but he wished to deter aggression.

Take note

Why might Kim and Stalin feel that the USA might not intervene?

Berlin Blockade

The Soviet Union closed all land links to Western-occupied West Berlin, which was within the Soviet sector of occupied Germany. It marked a considerable increase in Cold War tension. The British and Americans got round the blockade by a massive airlift. The blockade lasted from June 1948 to May 1949.

'A dagger pointed at the heart of Japan'

Japan was clearly a vital US interest and had been included within the essential US defence perimeter laid out in NSC 48 and in Acheson's speech of 12 January. Only 100 miles from Korea, and the major industrial producer in Asia, it was deemed essential to keep Japan friendly to the USA. A communist Korea could be considered a direct threat to US interests in Japan.

Acheson had immediately formed the opinion that the North Korean attack was orchestrated by Moscow and had to be resisted if further aggressive moves by Stalin were to be avoided. Truman was of the same opinion. Like all his generation, Acheson was conditioned by the events of the 1930s and the lead-up to the Second World War. If only Hitler and Mussolini had been confronted earlier when they made their first aggressive moves, then world war might have been averted. Stalin should be stopped and it was Stalin, not Kim Il Sung, who was seen as behind the attack. It seemed to fit a pattern of testing the West, most recently illustrated in the **Berlin Blockade**.

Dean Acheson had decided to involve the United Nations from the beginning, and on the day of the attack the Security Council adopted a resolution, nine votes to nil, to condemn the attack and call for North Korea's withdrawal from the South. Luckily for the USA, the Soviet Union had withdrawn its ambassador from the UN over the failure to recognise Mao's government as the legitimate government of China. This meant that the USSR could not exercise its right of veto.

On the evening of 25 June, a crucial meeting was held under Truman's chairmanship to decide the US response. Dean Rusk, the assistant secretary at the State Department, made the point that a Communist Korea would be **'a dagger pointed at the heart of Japan'**. Others stressed the need to draw a line at which it was necessary to resist Soviet aggression. General Bradley, head of the Joint Chiefs of Staff, argued that Korea was as good a place as any to draw the line, although Acheson was later to point out that of all the places to fight, Korea must have been the worst location in the world. It was a view with which large numbers of US and UN troops would sympathise. It was decided that the US would offer air and naval support and press for UN military support.

The decision to act gained unanimous support at the meeting and totally accorded with Truman's instincts. It was a view with which the vast majority of US citizens agreed. Truman received overwhelming support in the press, through letters and telegrams from the public and from Congress. The House of Representatives voted 315 to 4 to extend the draft law, enabling the government to call up young men to fight.

On 27 June the UN Security Council authorised the use of force to assist South Korea, and US forces would now act under a UN flag. When asked on the 29 June, at his first press conference since the North Korean attack, whether the US was at war, Truman denied it and described it as a 'police action under the United Nations'. The next day, when faced with MacArthur's request to deploy two US divisions to Korea, Truman immediately agreed. The US was at war in practice if not in theory.

Activity: Comparing North and South Korea

1. Draw up and complete a table comparing North and South Korea.

	North Korea	South Korea
Leader		
Ideology		
Patron state		
Army equipment		
Aircraft		

2. What were the significant differences between North Korea and South Korea?

3. For discussion: How far do you agree that the Korean War began because the USA failed to indicate that it would assist South Korea if it were attacked by the North?

Taking it further

For those wanting to take their study of Korea further there is a good history of modern Korea by Bruce Cummings, *Korea's Place in the Sun* (2005).

An excellent new study of the origins of the Korean War is to be found in *Rethinking the Korean War* by William Stueck (2002).

Chapter 3   The course of the Korean War

Key questions

- Why was North Korea initially so successful in 1950?
- How and why did the forces of the UN defeat North Korea in the autumn of 1950?
- Why and with what consequences did Chinese forces intervene?
- Why did President Truman dismiss General MacArthur in April 1950?

Why did the Korean War last so long?

The man who started the Korean War, Kim Il Sung, expected it to last only a few weeks. The USA did not consider it officially a war and consistently underestimated what was required. It turned into a vicious and bloody struggle lasting three years. To begin with there were dramatic changes of fortune, but from the spring of 1951 it became a bloody war of attrition, each side seeking victory by wearing the other down. It often appeared to be about to turn into a much broader struggle, which could have become a third world war with the widespread use of nuclear weapons.

Timeline

1950	**25 June:** North Korea invades South Korea
	July: First encounters of US troops with North Korean Army
	August/September: Fierce attacks on Pusan Perimeter
	15 September: Inchon landing outflanks North Korean forces
	October: Invasion of North Korea; Pyongyang captured Chinese launch limited offensive near border
	November: Massive Chinese attack on UN forces in North Korea
	December: Chinese move through North Korea and push south of the 38th parallel
	General Walker killed; replaced by General Matthew Ridgeway
1951	**January:** Chinese occupy Seoul
	February/March: Chinese advance stopped and forced back; Seoul recaptured
	April: MacArthur sacked as Supreme US Commander
	June: USA, Russia and China indicate willingness for ceasefire
1952	Lengthy arguments over prisoners hold up peace
	June: US begins heavy bombing of North Korea
	November: Eisenhower elected president
1953	**January:** Eisenhower takes over from Truman
	March: Stalin dies
	July: Armistice signed at Panmunjom

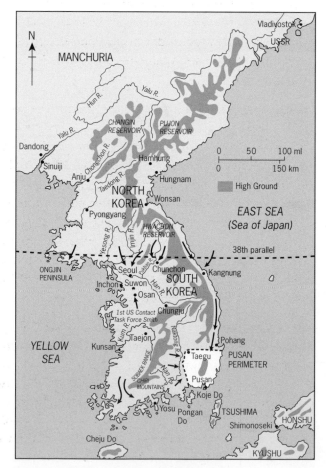

The North Korean attack, June 1950

The North Korean offensive, June–September 1950

At 4 am on the morning of 25 June, a devastating artillery and mortar barrage fell on unprepared South Korean troops. It rapidly became apparent that this was no tit-for-tat raid, the likes of which had been going on for nearly a year across the 38th parallel. Kim Il Sung was launching an all-out assault to reunite the peninsula. Seven well-equipped and well-motivated combat divisions with an armoured brigade of T-34 tanks poured across the border. They were supported by over 200 Russian-built aircraft. Three more freshly raised divisions were in support.

Kim commanded an army of 135,000 men. Nearly a third of them, and most of the officers and NCOs (non-commissioned officers), had extensive combat experience in the Chinese Civil War. It should have been a walkover. Kim anticipated the conquest to take three weeks – too quick for the USA to intervene and such intervention was not expected anyway.

The defenders

The South Korean forces by comparison were under-equipped, badly trained and badly led for the most part. The Republic of Korea (ROK) Army numbered approximately 95,000, considerably smaller than the North Korean Army. More importantly, it lacked tanks, anti-tank weapons and spare parts for its vehicles, a third of which were out of action awaiting repair. The ordinary soldiers were peasant conscripts with little love for their corrupt government or officers; they had little reason to fight. Often ROK units simply disintegrated under attack. Seoul, Syngman Rhee's capital, was taken on 29 June and it soon appeared possible that Kim would meet his target of a three-week war.

US forces were rushed to Korea to bolster the disintegrating ROK Army. The first to arrive, on 1 July, was the 24th Infantry Division from Japan. It was under-strength and inadequately trained, the weakest of MacArthur's forces. Much of its equipment was faulty and, like much of the US Army, it was a product of five years of low defence spending. It was said, but was untrue, that in some US units, slips of toilet paper were rationed to two per visit to the latrine. More seriously the 24th had bazookas that were totally ineffective against the T-34 tanks. MacArthur, who was appointed **US supreme commander** on 10 July, totally underestimated the strength of the North Korean attack and overestimated the impact of US troops. He was rapidly disabused of his complacency.

The 24th rushed into action south of Seoul and was forced into rapid retreat. The North Koreans tended to follow Chinese tactical doctrine, pressing round the sides of enemy units and finding a vulnerable flank to attack. US units tended to be tied to their vehicles and the limited road network; consequently they frequently found the enemy to their side and even their rear. Where a flank was supposedly guarded by ROK units, these often melted away. Panic among US troops was often the result and they adopted the response: 'bug out' – a disorderly retreat.

Take note

As you read through this section, take notes on the following points.
1. Why were the North Korean forces able to conquer so much of the South?
2. Why did they fail to capture Pusan?

Supreme commander

As supreme US commander, MacArthur was also appointed as the supreme UN commander but this position only arose because the USA was the dominant force in the UN coalition. It was the US president who sacked him in April 1951 and his US successor, General Matthew Ridgeway, then doubled up as supreme UN and US commander.

MacArthur appointed General Walton Walker to command the 8th US Army in Korea, based at the port of Pusan. The tough little Texan had his work cut out as the North Koreans pushed steadily south. He was reinforced by the 25th Infantry Division and 1st Cavalry Division, and more were on the way.

A Commonwealth brigade arrived from Hong Kong. Many regular British officers, like their senior American colleagues, were appalled at the inexperience of many US troops and their expectation of comfort level. Encouraged by the efficiency of the American supply system, US troops expected three good meals a day. A battalion of the Middlesex Regiment (a British unit), on arriving in Pusan, was amazed that their transport vehicles were loaded on to rail wagons only after ice-cream making machines had been moved north. Candy, coke, coffee and ice cream were deemed vital for US morale.

The tough and disciplined North Koreans knew none of these delights. Nevertheless, their advance south (without ice-cream making machines) presented them with increasing problems. The rugged countryside made supply difficult and the sheer fire power of the US air force and artillery began to tell. By early August the US and ROK forces had been forced back to a small pocket of South Korea in the south east of the peninsula, known as the Pusan Perimeter. Much of the strength of the position depended upon the line of the Naktong River.

At Pusan, Walker held the North Korean attacks in five weeks of bitter fighting. New and better bazookas began to arrive and the Pershing tank, which appeared in increasing numbers, could take out the T-34s. Overhead the USA had almost total command of the air, flown initially from a carrier force. The US and Commonwealth navies dominated the seas around Korea. Kim's dream of a three-week campaign had failed.

Furthermore, the sheer brutality of the North Korean troops and follow-up secret police began to produce a reaction in the South, which was ultimately to create a South Korean identity. Undoubtedly both sides committed atrocities. Syngman Rhee's police executed suspected communists, and British journalist, James Cameron, was so appalled that he questioned the British presence in the UN force. However, the brutalities of the South Korean

US prisoner shot with bound hands (barbed wire was often used)

authorities never matched those of the North. After the North Korean Army was forced back, 5000 bodies were discovered near the city of Taejon alone, and it has been estimated that Kim's forces killed 26,000 civilians in cold blood between June and September. Stalinist politics had arrived in the South, merciless and bloody. The corruption, inadequacies and cruelties of Rhee's regime were totally outclassed by the evils of Kim Il Sung. As is so often the case, the choice was not between good and evil but between a lesser evil and a greater one.

MacArthur's counterstroke, September 1950

Douglas MacArthur was 70 years old by 1950, balding and slightly deaf. Any other general of his age would have been pensioned off and certainly not appointed to head a complex modern war conducted by a UN coalition in the most inhospitable of environments. MacArthur, however, was not just an old general; he was a national institution, almost untouchable. He was seen as the man who had beaten the Japanese in the Pacific. His flair for publicity equalled his very considerable military ability and almost equalled his self-confidence. He despised politicians and Truman in particular. Generals, such as Eisenhower and Omar Bradley, now head of the Joint Chiefs of Staff (an influential group of US military leaders), had been his juniors in the thirties. Future President Eisenhower, when once asked if he knew MacArthur, replied that he had studied dramatics under him for many years.

General MacArthur – 'God's lieutenant'

As the ruler of conquered Japan since 1945, MacArthur behaved like an independent sovereign. Orders from Washington were treated merely as suggestions. His hold on the US press made it virtually impossible for him to be sacked. Already he had given Acheson and Truman real cause for concern with his desire to use Nationalist Chinese troops from Taiwan in the struggle in Korea. Chiang Kai-shek (Jiang Jieshi), the defeated Chinese leader, was anxious for his troops to be used; he was hoping to cause a Communist Chinese intervention in Korea and thus provoke a direct US–Chinese conflict, which he hoped would see him returned to the Chinese mainland. Acheson was determined to prevent this broadening of the war and, in the most unambiguous terms, got Truman to forbid the use of Chinese Nationalist soldiers. MacArthur reluctantly agreed to abide by the order.

The Inchon landing

The great man was, however, going to prove to the world that he really was the greatest of all military commanders by a daring stroke aimed at the North Koreans. His own staff in Tokyo treated him as a god and they were quickly won over by his plan for a landing at Inchon near Seoul. It was incredibly risky. There was a huge 30-foot (9-metre) daily tidal change and no beaches, merely glutinous mud. There was also the very real possibility that the North Koreans would mine the area.

Lieutenant General Edward Almond

(1892–1979)

Ned Almond was a devoted MacArthur man and served as his chief of staff. He was massively confident, ambitious and fanatically brave. He was determined to make the reputation in the Korean War that he felt fate had denied him unjustly in the Second World War. He clashed temperamentally with the cautious commander of the marine division in his corps, Oliver P. Smith.

Glossary: China lobby

This was a powerful group in the USA who supported Chiang Kai-shek (Jiang Jieshi) and felt that Truman's government should have done more to assist the Chinese Nationalists during the civil war. It included several Republican politicians and Henry Luce, the publisher of the influential *Time* and *Life* magazines.

However, MacArthur was certain that the landing at Inchon would work and convinced the reluctant Joint Chiefs of Staff to let the operation go ahead. He promised that Seoul would be liberated within three months of the start of the war. The date for the invasion was set for 15 September. MacArthur placed his favourite courtier from Tokyo, **Lieutenant General Edward Almond**, in command of the invasion corps, including the 1st Marine Division to spearhead the assault. Amazingly, Kim was taken completely by surprise. The harbour had not been mined despite advice from the government of Mao that it was a likely US move. The operation went like a dream, and with minimal casualties Inchon was taken. The US forces then pressed on to Seoul. Here, there was bitter fighting as the North Koreans had rushed in reinforcements. The marines were urged to make rapid progress despite casualties. MacArthur and Almond were determined to meet the three-month promise of liberation to impress the media. Massive bombing was used and the destruction of the city resulted. MacArthur flew from Japan into Kimpo airport near Seoul to pose for the appropriate pictures.

It appeared MacArthur truly was a genius as the whole North Korean position in South Korea collapsed. Walker's army in the Pusan Perimeter broke out to drive the fleeing remnants of the North Korean invaders before them. Kim's army faced the possibility of annihilation with the landing at Inchon. Cut off from its supplies, threatened by massive US air power and badly weakened by its repeated attacks on Walker's army in August and early September, it scrambled as best it could back north of the 38th parallel. Kim's gamble in trying to seize the whole of Korea had turned into disaster. Now MacArthur hoped he could 'liberate' the whole of Korea. After his victory at Inchon he was more than ever untouchable and difficult to control.

The decision to move north of the 38th parallel

The risks of China's involvement in Korea

There were clearly risks involved in moving into North Korea. The greatest danger was that it would provoke Chinese intervention. There were already large numbers of Chinese divisions in Manchuria, just north of the Yalu River that marked the border. To occupy the whole of Korea would bring US forces to the Yalu and, in the north east, to the border with the Soviet Union. On 1 October, some ROK units crossed the 38th parallel into North Korea. On 2 October, at midnight, Zhou Enlai, the Chinese prime minister, suddenly summoned the Indian ambassador in Beijing to tell him that if US forces crossed the border, China would be forced to intervene. The Chinese hoped that India would pass the message on to the USA since there were no direct diplomatic links between the People's Republic of China and the USA. Unfortunately the State Department did not take the warning seriously. MacArthur was convinced that the Chinese would not intervene and was determined to complete his triumph of Inchon by 'rolling back communism' from North Korea. He enjoyed enormous support within the USA from the general public and in particular from the **'China lobby'**, who actually welcomed a conflict with Mao's China, hoping it would see the return of Chiang Kai-shek (Jiang Jieshi) and a reversal of what they saw as the humiliating defeat of 1949.

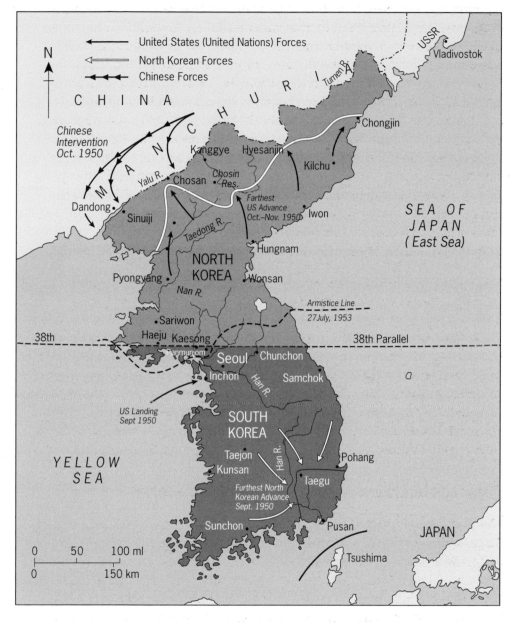

The UN counter-attack, September–November 1950

The American decision to invade North Korea

In the circumstances of 1950, it is not difficult to see why Truman and the State Department found it impossible to resist the pressure to invade the North. Militarily it made little sense to stop at the arbitrary line of the 38th parallel. Why stop and then wait for the North to recover and then attack again? It was thought far better to push on and either eliminate the threat from the North totally or at least find a better defensive line further north on which to dig in and defend. Morally, they felt that the Soviet Union had lost credibility and destroyed the sanctity of the 1945 agreements by sanctioning and encouraging Kim's assault. In other words, they started it so must now take the consequences and accept the loss of North Korea from their sphere of influence.

> **Take note**
>
> As you read through this section, identify all the different factors which led the USA to cross the 38th parallel.

George Kennan

(1904–2005)

Influential US diplomat who shaped American policy in the early days of the Cold War. In many ways he should be seen as the godfather of the policy of 'containment', but he opposed the move north of the 38th parallel and later was an opponent of greater involvement in Vietnam.

Within the State Department, the moderates, such as **George Kennan**, who saw the Soviet Union as badly behaved but containable, were being replaced by more aggressive Cold War warriors like Dean Rusk, John Allison and John Foster Dulles. To this new group, it was essential to respond to challenges from Moscow with a hard-hitting response in order to discourage such adventures. There was a growing anti-communist lobby in the USA, most notably enshrined in the singularly unpleasant and unprincipled figure of Senator Joe McCarthy, but even moderate Republicans were pressing for a tougher line on Moscow. Public opinion seemed to be behind this tougher stance and opinion polls indicated that 64 per cent of American citizens favoured invading the North. Since Congressional elections were due in November it is little wonder that Truman and Acheson found it almost impossible to resist the pressure to cross the 38th parallel, although they indicated in the orders issued to MacArthur that he should show restraint. He was not to undertake any act which risked extending the war to conflict with either China or the USSR. US troops were not to be used near the border. Despite these warnings, the orders given to the supreme commander were ambiguous, and knowing MacArthur's tendency to interpret any order in a way that suited him, they offered little real restraint.

Even apart from the possibility of Chinese intervention, there were real problems of supply and communication in invading North Korea. Winter was approaching and sub-arctic temperatures of minus 30 degrees Celsius were likely. Roads were few and the country was divided by a central mountainous spine, which would divide the forces: in the west under Walker from 10th Corps and in the east under Almond. MacArthur brushed aside all problems, insisting that the North Koreans were beaten and the Chinese would not intervene. He was badly served by his sycophantic head of intelligence, Major General Willoughby. Willoughby knew what MacArthur wanted to be told and made sure the intelligence fitted the bill. The numbers of Chinese troops in Manchuria was consistently underestimated, as was their quality. To MacArthur, the war was nearly over apart from a parade to the Yalu River.

To add to his glory, MacArthur hoped to pull off the odd sensation for the press, such as the planned landing at the port of Wonsan, a repeat of the Inchon landings but on the other side of the peninsula and further north. This time, however, the result was a farce. The harbour had been mined by the North Koreans and US troops were left out at sea waiting for minesweepers. By the time the harbour was clear, the port had been taken by UN forces from the land and the comedian Bob Hope, who had arrived to entertain the troops, was actually waiting in Wonsan for the would-be US invaders.

By the end of October, the narrowest point in the Korean Peninsula had been reached. It was only a hundred miles from the port of Chongju, in the west, which had been taken by the British Commonwealth Brigade, to the port of Hungnam in the east. This was the obvious place to stop and draw a defensive line. Only the really desolate and mountainous border region remained and Kim could have been left with a rump state, protecting Chinese and Russian interests.

MacArthur was having none of this approach, which he felt was appeasing communism. He ordered his ground commanders to advance to the Yalu. Almond responded with enthusiasm; Walker more cautiously. Walker was wise to do so. On 1–2 November, as if from nowhere, a large force of Chinese troops struck an elite force of his troops at Unsan, 50 miles south of the border. They inflicted a terrible battering on the Americans and swept away several ROK units on their flanks. Over 150,000 Chinese troops had crossed into Korea and Willoughby's intelligence knew nothing of it. Attacks were also launched on Almond's force in the east, which the marines beat off but took casualties.

At the end of the first week in November the Chinese broke off their attacks and seemed to withdraw into the border hills. Was this a final warning to the UN not to press on, as some think, or a calculated trick to draw the US on? Mao had been briefed in October on the character of MacArthur, who was described to him as arrogant. Mao is reported to have been pleased because 'such men were easy to defeat'. The commander of the Chinese 9th Army group put the same point in typical peasant fashion: 'To catch a big fish, you must first let the fish taste your bait.' The Chinese were drawing MacArthur on. He fell for it and took the bait, ordering his forces further north into ever more inhospitable terrain. He was convinced the Chinese had been beaten off. Even though Willoughby now had to admit the presence of Chinese forces, he still massively underestimated their numbers. The USA was walking into one of the greatest ambushes of all time.

The impact of China's involvement in the war

China's intervention was of massive significance. There was a real possibility of it triggering a third world war, which could be the world's first nuclear war. Such an eventuality was avoided but at the very least it ended dreams of a reunited Korea and ensured that the war, which MacArthur was certain would be over by Christmas, would drag on into 1953.

Why did China intervene?

The decision to intervene was not taken lightly by the **Chinese Politburo**. China was ravaged by years of warfare and the Chinese Communist regime still struggled to assert its authority and control, particularly in the south. Chiang Kai-shek (Jiang Jieshi) had withdrawn to Taiwan with a formidable army and this was the priority target for most of the Chinese leadership. The USA seemed to have abandoned Chiang until North Korea struck south. At that point Truman reversed US policy and sent the 7th US Fleet to patrol between Taiwan and the mainland, making a Communist invasion impossible. This infuriated some of the Chinese leaders, as did the American denial of Communist China's membership of the United Nations between 1949 and 1979. However, whether confrontation with the strongest power in the world was advisable was another matter.

Take note

As you read through this section, list the reasons for Chinese intervention in Korea. What risks was Mao running by intervening?

Chinese Politburo

As in the Soviet Union, the key decision-making body was called the 'Politburo'. It was the policy committee of the governing Communist Party. Mao Zedong was the senior figure and chairman of the Communist Party, with Liu Shoqui as number 2 and Zhou Enlai as number 3. Other important figures included the Communist Party secretary, Deng Xiao Ping, and the military men, Peng Dehuai and Lin Biao.

Peng Dehuai

(1898–1974)

Peng was a tough Communist military veteran. He had led one of the two columns during the Long March of 1934–35, when the Communists had rebased themselves in the inhospitable north west. He respected Mao as the political leader but was not afraid to speak his mind. Following the Korean War he realised that Mao's faith in the courage, endurance and commitment of the People's Liberation Army (PLA) was not enough against modern Western technology; he recognised that the PLA needed to be transformed into a professional force. He eventually clashed seriously with Mao and was arrested and tortured to death during the Cultural Revolution.

Take note

What factors made it possible for Chinese forces to reach Seoul?
Draw a diagram with 'In January 1951 the Chinese occupied Seoul' in the centre of the circle.
Place your factors around the circle, adding key points to show their significance.
Draw arrows to indicate links between them and to the statement in the centre.
Label the arrows to explain the links you have made.

Stalin pressed the Chinese to assist Kim, but it was plain that direct Soviet intervention was out of the question. The best that could be hoped for was air cover, which Stalin promised. Many of the Chinese leaders, including Mao, distrusted the Soviet Union and could see that they wished to use China for their own benefit. Mao, nevertheless, could recognise arguments for intervention. He did not want hostile US forces on the border with Chinese Manchuria, where most of China's limited industry was concentrated. This industry depended in part on electricity generated by hydroelectric power in North Korea. Furthermore, Mao could see that a conflict could heighten nationalist sentiment in China behind the new regime, helping him to sweep away enemies and impose his programme of reform. He was also very conscious of Chinese history. As it had for his hero, the first emperor of China, a successful foreign adventure could consolidate Mao's power and prestige. The first Qin emperor had invaded Vietnam in the 3rd century BC; for Mao, that other traditional tributary province of China would do – Korea.

Mao appears to have had a hard time convincing his Politburo colleagues. The obvious choice to command the armies, Lin Biao, hero of the civil war fighting in Manchuria, refused to support war. Zhou Enlai, the prime minister, was half-hearted, but he had learned not to oppose Mao directly. Mao's greatest ally proved to be China's other great soldier, **Peng Dehuai**, a hero of the fabled 'Long March' of 1934. He supported intervention and was appointed to command the 300,000 troops that China began to assemble on the Korean border. The decision was taken in October to intervene, since the USA had crossed the 38th parallel.

The 'dragon' attacks

The Chinese armies now poised on the border of North Korea were very different from those of the USA. They were essentially tough but lightly armed infantry. They were not limited to the roads, having little mechanical transport. Their artillery could not match that of the USA and they relied largely on rifles, machine guns and mortars. There was little Soviet air support, despite Mao's hopes of Stalin's promises. The Chinese troops were, however, masters of camouflage and the surprise attack. Clad in quilted cotton jackets and light shoes, they could move quickly through difficult terrain. They appreciated the importance of air power and their lack of it, and therefore moved mostly at night, often launching their attacks in the hours of darkness. They lacked modern methods of communication, namely radios, and relied on, what were to Western ears, a weird collection of sounds to convey orders. The noise from trumpets, gongs and other musical instruments filled the air and often caused the hair on the backs of Western necks to stand on end. In short, two alien cultures confronted one another.

By mid-November, between 120,000 and 150,000 Chinese troops confronted Almond's 10th Corps in the east, and considerably more than this, in excess of 200,000, faced Walker's 8th Army in the west. The trap was about to be sprung. Almond, echoing MacArthur's confidence and believing Willoughby's low estimates, urged the Marine Division north up an 80-mile (128 km)

The 'dragon' attacks; US marines
in retreat from Chosin

single-track road to the Chosin Reservoir near the border. The marines'
commander suspected a trap, as a crucial bridge over a chasm had not been
blown up by retreating Communist forces, but he reluctantly obeyed orders
and advanced his highly trained 20,000 men northward into the icy hills.

On 25 November, the Chinese offensive against Walker in the west began
near the town of Kunuri. The UN front collapsed. ROK units broke and fled,
and US forces faced being surrounded. The decision was taken to retreat.
Thus the longest retreat in US military history began – 300 miles (480 km)
in total. Units pulled back with increasing rapidity. Morale plummeted and
it became increasingly impossible to think of making a stand to halt the
Chinese advance.

In the east it looked as if a bigger disaster was brewing. The attack there
began two days later, on 27 November. By this time nearly 100,000 Chinese
veterans had encircled the Marine Corps, blocking its retreat from the Chosin
Reservoir. In this case, the encirclement failed and the marines proceeded
to blast their way down the road they had only two weeks before advanced
up. It was a feat of tight discipline and incredible fire power. When asked if
he was retreating, the US marine commander replied that he was merely
advancing in a different direction. The Chinese now blew the bridge over
the chasm to halt the marines but bridging equipment was flown in from
Japan and guns, tanks and vehicles of all sorts passed down the road to the
port of Hungham. Almond's whole corps then embarked with little loss of

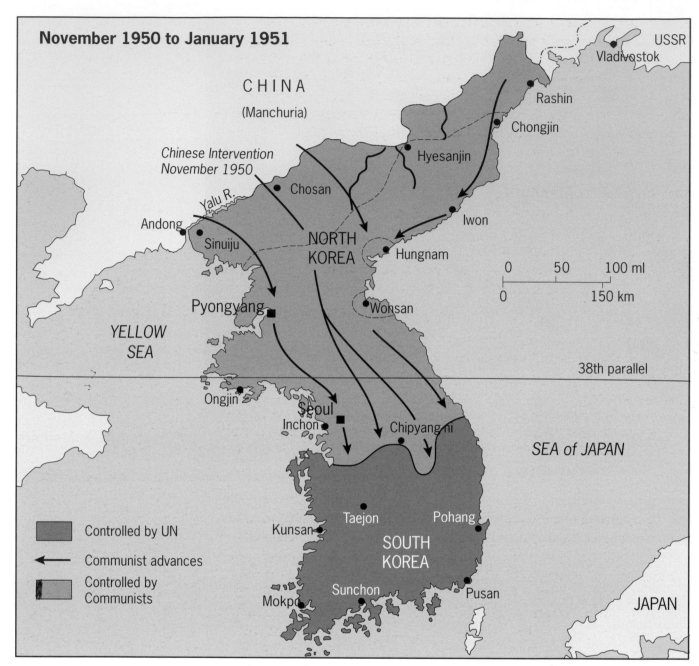

November 1950 to January 1951

USSR

Vladivostok

CHINA
(Manchuria)

Rashin

Chongjin

*Chinese Intervention
November 1950*

Hyesanjin

Chosan

Yalu R.

Iwon

Andong

Sinuiju

NORTH
KOREA

Hungnam

Pyongyang

Wonsan

YELLOW
SEA

0   50   100 ml

0   150 km

38th parallel

Ongjin

Seoul

Inchon

Chipyang-ni

SEA of JAPAN

Taejon

Pohang

Kunsan

SOUTH
KOREA

Mokpo

Sunchon

Pusan

JAPAN

Controlled by UN

Communist advances

Controlled by
Communists

The dragon strikes: the
Chinese advance, November
1950–January 1951

men, equipment or even accompanying civilian refugees. It was a triumph
of naval and air power. It was impossible to remain in the north east as the
western front had collapsed, and even MacArthur had to accept the logic of
this, although blaming others for the disaster.

The northern capital of Pyongyang was abandoned and thousands of tons of
stores destroyed. On 23 December, Walker was killed in a road accident. His
replacement was Matthew Ridgeway, an eminent paratroop commander, and
although he could not instantly stop the retreat he first slowed it and began
to try to restore morale. Nevertheless, Seoul was lost for the second time, and
it was not until some 50 miles (80 km) to the south that the Chinese were
finally halted. They had outrun their supplies and were hungry, frozen and
pounded from the air by a massively superior US air power. In this way the
great retreat came to an end in February 1951.

Intervention in Korea had taken a terrible toll on Chinese lives. The appalling fire power of a unit like the Marine Division impressed Peng, who had become much more cautious than Kim Il Sung or Mao. In March, Ridgeway was able to launch an offensive, which pushed the Communist forces back and recaptured Seoul. MacArthur flew into Korea to take the limelight and claim that he had ordered the offensive, which in reality he had had little to do with. The truth was that MacArthur was not only irritating Ridgeway; he was increasingly infuriating Washington.

The sacking of MacArthur

Truman had never liked MacArthur, detesting his inflated ego. On flying to visit him in October 1950, he wrote to a friend that he was going to see 'God's right-hand man'. The feeling was mutual and 'God's right-hand man' detested Truman. When they met on 15 October, MacArthur refused to salute his commander-in-chief, as custom would indicate he should.

In December 1950, as MacArthur's triumphal conquest of North Korea collapsed in ruins, he gave an interview to an American journal blaming the restraints put upon him for the retreat. He had not been able to bomb Chinese bases in Manchuria and he blamed America's European allies for imposing the restraints. The interview outraged Truman and Acheson; it was completely inappropriate for a serving soldier to question high-level decision making in this public fashion. Truman would have sacked MacArthur then had the situation not been so serious. Instead, he was merely told not to repeat such flagrant breaches of etiquette.

Then, on 15 March 1951, the day after Seoul was retaken, MacArthur issued a press statement that the unification of the entire peninsula was still his goal – in other words, he sought total victory. Already Truman and Acheson had decided to settle for a return to the 38th parallel. MacArthur, however, was urging on Washington the need to extend bombing to Manchuria and poison the Yalu River boundary with radioactive waste to cut off Korea from China. Such requests were firmly denied. Truman informed MacArthur on the 20 March that the USA was going to propose a ceasefire along the 38th parallel. This infuriated the general, who considered it appeasement, and he deliberately sabotaged it in his own communiqué, which insulted the Chinese and threatened to extend the war to their territory. Truman reprimanded him but still did not act. His approval ratings as president had fallen to 26 per cent in a recent poll, while MacArthur still basked in popular adulation.

The last straw came when, in direct contradiction of all the warnings he had received, MacArthur sent a letter to the leader of the Republicans in the House of Representatives, Joe Martin, which was read out on 5 April. It claimed that 'there was no substitute for victory' (the conquest of the whole of Korea) and that Nationalist troops from Taiwan should be used. It forced Truman to act. MacArthur was challenging the civilian government's control of policy making and proposing a course of action which would lead, as he intended, to a full-scale war with China. Such a course was totally unacceptable to both Truman and Acheson, and in particular to their British

Take note

As you read though this section:
1. List the reasons for the sacking of MacArthur.
2. Make notes on why the sacking of MacArthur was so risky for Truman.

Glossary:

Impeach

A judicial process, provided for in the US Constitution, for the removal of US public officials including the president. A two-thirds majority in the Senate is required for conviction. Andrew Johnson, president in succession to Abraham Lincoln, was impeached but narrowly acquitted. The threat of impeachment led Nixon to resign in August 1974. President Clinton was also impeached in 2000.

The 'Glorious Glosters'

The US command credited this British brigade with saving Seoul. Although the Gloucestershire battalion was wiped out by death and capture, possibly 10,000 Chinese troops were killed or wounded. The failure to order the Glosters to withdraw at the appropriate moment arose from the Americans' failure to appreciate British understatement. On being asked by his US superior for a situation report, the commander of the Glosters admitted to it being 'somewhat sticky'. He was told to hold. Running out of ammunition eventually, the battalion was forced to surrender.

allies, who had recently stressed the need not to extend the war. On 11 April MacArthur was fired.

It was politically a very brave but necessary decision. As Truman expected, there were howls of protest. There was talk among Republicans of **impeaching** the president. The young Republican senator for California, Richard Nixon, demanded MacArthur's immediate reinstatement. Two thousand dockers in New York staged a protest walk out. Telegrams and letters poured into the White House denouncing the sacking. A Gallup Poll (public opinion survey) indicated that 69 per cent backed MacArthur. The process reached a crescendo on MacArthur's return, when 10,000 welcomed him at San Francisco airport.

On 19 April, MacArthur addressed Congress. It was televised and a record 30 million tuned in to watch. MacArthur was at his brilliant melodramatic best. He was the victim of appeasement, he claimed, and America was surrendering to Communist aggression. Republican Representative Short of Missouri claimed that he had heard God speak. Clearly MacArthur was no longer merely 'God's right-hand man'; he was the deity himself. Truman dismissed the whole speech as 'bullshit'. The next day a reputed 7.5 million turned out in New York to shout their approval of MacArthur in a ticker-tape parade.

Yet slowly, as Truman had predicted, the excitement began to subside. Initially the more thoughtful Republicans and the well-informed professionals in the press backed the president. A series of hearings before the Senate Foreign Relations and Armed Services Committee helped turn the tide, as the senior military figures of the Joint Chiefs of Staff and General Marshall, the secretary for defense, threw their weight behind the president. General Bradley famously denounced the widening of the war to China as involving the USA in 'the wrong war, at the wrong place, at the wrong time, and with the wrong enemy'.

The end of the Korean War

The USA had decided in March 1951 to seek an armistice on or around the 38th parallel. It appears that Peng, the Chinese commander, had reached the same conclusion, although Mao Zedong had not as yet; under pressure from Kim and Stalin, he agreed to a further 'Spring Offensive' to recapture Seoul. The result was a series of bloody actions to the north of the South Korean capital. Prominent among the resisters was the British Commonwealth Brigade and the heroic stand of the '**Glorious Glosters**'. The defeat of the Chinese offensive convinced even Mao that a ceasefire might be desirable and yet the war was to last another two years.

Armistice negotiations

The first armistice negotiations were held at Kaesong in July 1951 but turned into something of a fiasco. The Communists used it as a propaganda exercise to imply that the USA was pleading for peace. Kim was certainly still opposed to a deal and so it appears was Stalin, who felt that a bubbling conflict would occupy and weaken the USA and tie China more firmly to the USSR. There were endless procedural matters and saving face was vital. The UN delegation placed a small UN flag in front of where they were sitting so the Communist delegation placed a larger flag in front of their position.

The talks were moved in the autumn to the little village of Panmunjom, where they would continue on and off until 27 July 1953. There were endless sticking points over the exact boundary and, most importantly, over the issue of the return of prisoners. Truman was adamant that he would not force Communist prisoners to return against their will. He was very conscious of the brutal treatment meted out by the USSR to returned prisoners at the end of the Second World War.

Meanwhile, the war continued as a largely static war of attrition reminiscent of the trench warfare of the First World War. The Chinese and North Koreans tunnelled and dug in and the UN poured down upon them volleys of artillery fire. A new horrific weapon, napalm, was developed to clear Chinese bunkers. Horrific fireballs of burning sticky chemicals used up the oxygen for yards around, asphyxiating victims at a distance and horribly burning and mutilating those with whom it came in contact. North Korea was endlessly bombed to make them sign an armistice. Eventually, following Stalin's death in March 1953 and the arrival in Washington of a new Republican administration under Eisenhower, whom the Communists feared might be more aggressive, a ceasefire was signed (but not a peace treaty).

Activity: Speech writing

Write two brief speeches of no more than one side of A4:

1. as Truman justifying MacArthur's sacking
2. as MacArthur arguing for extending the war and 'liberating' North Korea.

As Truman, try to capture his simple, direct approach. An appropriate word to describe this approach is 'laconic', i.e. nothing fancy and elaborate.

As MacArthur, try to capture his 'grandiloquent' style full of flourish and bombast. He was said to speak rather like a Victorian actor with exaggerated phrases and gestures.

Taking it further

There are many accounts of the Korean War. Two British accounts which focus on the relatively small British contribution are:

- *The Korean War* by M. Hickey (1999)
- *The Korean War* by M. Hastings (1987).

The best recent American narrative account of the Korean War is *The Coldest Winter* by D. Halberstam (2007).

To get a sense of differing American perspectives on the war, two outstanding biographies are:

- *Truman* by D. McCullough (1992), which gives the president's view of events
- *American Caesar: Douglas MacArthur 1880–1964* by W. Manchester (1979).

Debate this question: should the USA have extended the war to China and re-conquered North Korea in 1951?

Chapter 4   The consequences of the Korean War

Key questions

- What was the impact on Korea?
- What was the impact on Japan?
- What were the consequences for China?
- What were the consequences for the USA?

The Korean War obviously had devastating consequences for the people of both North and South Korea in the short term. In the long term it also determined that the two countries would develop very differently and had repercussions far outside the Korean peninsula. It was a major event in both post-war international relations and American and Chinese domestic politics. It influenced US policy in Asia for years to come and gave the United Nations a credibility which its predecessor, the League of Nations, had lacked.

Take note

Identify the short- and long-term effects of the war on each country.

	Short-term impact	Long-term impact
Korea		
Japan		
China		
USA		

Timeline

1950	**June:** First US supplies reach the French in Vietnam Increasing number of US orders for Japanese industry
1951	US–Japanese Security Treaty. Formal peace treaty signed Seven CIA stations established abroad
1952	Anti-communist paranoia at its height in USA **November:** Eisenhower elected president
1953	**January:** John Foster Dulles appointed secretary of state 47 CIA stations abroad Japan creates Self Defence Force
1954	**January:** Defensive treaty between South Korea and USA ratified by Senate

The impact of the war on Korea

To the USA and the rest of the world, the Korean War was a 'limited war'. Truman had called it a 'police action', and the Chinese had sent in 'volunteers' and were not formally at war with the USA. To the Koreans it was a total war. The suffering and devastation was horrendous. Possibly 10 per cent of the entire Korean population was reported as killed, wounded or missing. About 600,000 homes were destroyed in North Korea and South Korea combined. In the North alone, 8700 industrial plants were knocked out, largely through repeated US bombing. The civilian population of the North declined from 9 million to 7 million through death and emigration. The Republic of Korea Army lost 415,000 killed and 429,000 wounded. Despite the ambitions of Syngman Rhee and Kim Il Sung to reunify the peninsula, it has remained divided, roughly along the line that existed in June 1950. In this sense, the war was a futile tragedy.

The two Koreas, however, developed differently. Neither had any democratic tradition and they were poor, undeveloped 'Third World' countries in 1950.

- North Korea has essentially remained what it was in 1950: a brutal, primitive dictatorship with a low standard of living. Its patrons, China and Russia, have changed dramatically, Russia abandoning communism in theory and practice and China simply abandoning it in practice. (In both cases this has been to the benefit of economic development.) North Korea remains locked in a Stalinist time warp, sealed off from the twenty-first century.

- South Korea remained an authoritarian state for many years, first under Rhee, until his removal in 1960, and then under the army. The US agreed to offer South Korea protection and based troops there but insisted there should be no attacks on North Korea. Slowly democracy developed, with a growing middle class and prosperity. The South Korea of the late twentieth century, it could be argued, justified the war and fulfilled the hopes of Truman and the UN.

The impact on Japan

Japan, as the major industrial power of Asia, was a much more vital interest to the USA than Korea. It was probably the major beneficiary of the Korean War. Not only was a friendly South Korea established, just a hundred miles from Japan's shores, instead of a hostile puppet regime of the Soviet Union, but Japan also gained enormously from US spending on the war. Japan was the key base for all operations and the recipient of much direct US defence spending. Toyota received an order in July 1950 from the USA for 1000 trucks, more than three times its production of the previous month. By 1954, the Japanese defence industry earned 3 billion US dollars from sales.

The Korean War was therefore a massive stimulus to the economic recovery of Japan and contributed to the prosperity that underpinned its fledgling democracy. It helped create a rich, friendly state that in many ways was the cornerstone of US interests in the region. The USA underlined this by signing a security pact with Japan in 1951 and persuading the Japanese to begin, at least, a partial rearmament as a defence against Soviet and Chinese power. The Japanese prime minister, Yoshida, claimed that the war was 'the grace of heaven', so beneficial had it been to Japan.

The impact on the People's Republic of China
Human cost

As with Korea, the human cost to China of the Korean War was enormous. Over 150,000 troops were killed and many times this figure were wounded. The sheer fire power of the US-led coalition was something never encountered in the People's Liberation Army's long struggle with Japan and the Chinese Nationalists. It convinced Peng Dehuai that China could not win by sheer numbers and political enthusiasm alone. He realised that a new, more technological army was needed, and he set about trying to create this over the next few years.

> **Take note**
>
> Why can it be argued that the impact on Japan was almost wholly beneficial?

Economic cost

The economic cost of the war, despite some aid from the Soviet Union, was also a crushing burden on a poor country. It slowed up the new Communist regime's drive to modernise China. The war had also prevented the complete defeat of the Nationalists, safely screaming defiance at the Communists from Taiwan. They were now protected by the US 7th Fleet and there was little prospect of final and complete victory for Mao over Chiang Kai-shek (Jiang Jieshi). The USA even proposed to defend the offshore islands of Quemoy and Matsu, which were precariously held by the Nationalists, and this was to produce confrontation at various times, particularly in 1954. Furthermore, US hostility to Communist China was now greater than ever and would ensure Communist China's continued exclusion from membership of the UN.

Success for China

On the other hand, Mao saw the war as a success on balance. Communist China really had stood up to the outside world, as he promised it would do when he proclaimed the People's Republic in October 1949. China had taken on the most powerful country in the world and forced it back, restoring a friendly buffer state between China and the hostile West. Furthermore, the war had helped to consolidate the regime's hold on power in China, and Mao's authority in particular. Many of the tiny elite of the Western-educated in China, who traditionally looked to the USA, had been disciplined and repressed. The war had justified repression and the removal of all those who might challenge the new regime. For such an achievement it was a small price in blood to pay; Mao always thought on the grand scale and a few hundred thousand lives were not really significant. A victorious campaign was the mark of a new dynasty and a new emperor. Like his hero, the first emperor in the 3rd century BC who had made his mark in Vietnam, Mao had made his mark in Korea.

The impact on the United States
Human and economic cost

For the USA, the human cost of the war was certainly less than it was for China, but it was not insignificant: 33,651 Americans died in combat and a further 103,284 were wounded. For a limited 'police action' this was surprising. The financial implications were also shocking for the US treasury. Total military expenditure rose from a mere 4 per cent of GNP in 1948 to 14 per cent of GNP by 1953. It was a very expensive 'police action'. The USA had also suffered a humiliating military setback in December 1950, retreating 300 miles (483 km) in the face of under-armed Chinese soldiers. In all these ways the war might be considered a disaster for America.

Anti-communist paranoia

The war also encouraged the anti-communist paranoia that had been developing throughout the late 1940s. Senator Joseph McCarthy went from strength to strength in 1950–1951, denouncing hidden plots that stretched to the White House. The State Department under Acheson was a particular target for his denunciations but so too (unbelievably to any sane US citizen) was General Marshall, now Truman's secretary of defense. Few real spies or communist subversives were ever uncovered, but McCarthy became a feared presence in American politics, undermining the Democrat administration. The senior figures in the Republican Party went along with McCarthy while Truman was in office, but when **Eisenhower**, himself a Republican, became president in 1953, McCarthy became an embarrassment to them and in 1954 faded into alcoholic oblivion.

Eisenhower 'I will go to Korea'

Korea had undoubtedly helped Eisenhower to the White House. He was selected as the Republican Party's candidate despite having few political connections until this point. He was safely conservative and seen as pleasant by all. Without spelling out how he would do it, he implied that he would end the Korean War, which by 1952 was increasingly unpopular. His speechwriters, desperate for an election-winning headline, came up with the phrase 'I will go to Korea'. What he would do when he got there was not spelled out and no one asked this difficult question. It was sufficient that the general who had conquered Germany would go to Korea. Eisenhower did indeed go to Korea after his

'Vote for Ike' cartoon by Cummings, Daily Express 6 November 1952

election victory, talked briefly to the senior US figures there and returned to the United States with no clearer idea than Truman as to how to end the war. Luckily, Stalin died on 6 March, just weeks after Eisenhower's **inauguration** on 20 January, and all three communist states decided to call it a day. Eisenhower had been lucky.

Increase in defence spending

The biggest impact on the USA was the vast increase in defence spending and the transformation of the American nation from an economic superpower into a military one. NSC 68, the proposal from the National Security Council to increase the USA's military spending (see Chapter 1, page 8), was now carried out. Before the Korean War broke out, the president, let alone Congress, had been unwilling to accept the suggestions of the State Department as to what the USA should spend on defence to look after its interests in the world. Under the impact of war, however, dollars flowed into the armed services. The number of the navy's ships rose from 600 to 1000; the air force increased from 42 wing groups to 72; the army grew from 10 to 18 divisions. The number of atomic bombs rocketed, from 300 in 1950 to 800 in 1952. Covert operations also received an enormous boost. **The CIA**, established only in 1948, expanded rapidly – there had been only seven overseas stations in 1951; by early 1953 there were 47. The USA really was equipping itself to be the world's policeman, even if this role was

Dwight Eisenhower

(1890–1969)

Eisenhower had been selected by General Marshall, the senior US military planner during the Second World War, to take command of US forces, first in North Africa and then for the invasion of France in 1944. He had little battle experience but was a superb diplomat and organiser. The defeat of Germany made him a national celebrity and he was immediately talked of as a future presidential candidate. He had no strong party loyalties but was a moderate conservative and agreed to stand as a Republican in the 1952 election.

Glossary:

Inauguration

American presidents are elected in November but do not take over until the following January, when they take the oath of office in an 'inauguration' ceremony. It is a form of coronation.

The CIA

The Central Intelligence Agency is the US equivalent of MI6 in Britain – a national security organisation for the gathering of strategic intelligence and the planning and execution of 'covert' (secret) operations to further US interests round the world.

not consciously embraced. At home the effect of this was to stimulate the economy and add to prosperity, but at the expense of cutting some welfare programmes that Truman had christened the 'Fair Deal.' Defence industries boomed and what Eisenhower was to later call the military-industrial complex was born.

American commitments in Asia

In Asia, as in Europe, American commitments multiplied. Kim, with Stalin's blessing, had prodded the USA into a confrontation that the communist states were ill prepared to match. Taiwan, Japan and South Korea were all now guaranteed by treaty and US troops were stationed appropriately. The USA had shown that it was prepared to fight and the world would not forget it.

UN credibility

The United Nations had also received a shot of credibility. It had not gone down the same ineffectual path as the League of Nations in the 1930s. Many powers had joined the USA in the fight against North Korea – the United Kingdom, Turkey, Canada, Colombia, Australia, South Africa, Greece, the Netherlands, France, Belgium, the Philippines and New Zealand. Truman's government had shown a determination to resist aggression but had chosen to do so under an international umbrella. It had embraced morality and deliberately eschewed relying simply on its own strength. Undoubtedly the USA could have inflicted grievous damage on China, possibly bringing down the Communist regime, but MacArthur's strategy was rejected and he was sacked. A limited war with allies was pursued instead of a sweeping US victory.

Containment of communism

Nevertheless, there was a determination to contain the spread of communism, which was seen as controlled from Moscow. Help began to flow ever more generously to the French in Indo-China and the seeds were planted for what became the USA's involvement in Vietnam.

Activity

Taking it further

Debate: 'The Korean War showed that the United Nations had teeth and gave it credibility.'

List the gains and losses of the Korean War for each of the following countries and decide whether the conflict was a victory or defeat for them:

- North Korea
- South Korea
- USA
- China
- USSR.

Skills Builder 1: **Writing in paragraphs**

In the examination you will have to write an essay-style answer on Conflict in Asia, in approximately 40 minutes. When producing an essay-style answer, it is important that you write in paragraphs. You will need to make a number of points to build up your argument so that it answers the question you have been asked. You should write a paragraph to address each point.

What should you include in a paragraph?

In a paragraph you should:

- Make a point to support your argument and answer the question

- Provide evidence to support your point

- Explain how your evidence supports your point

- Explain how your points relate to the essay question.

Remember: POINT – EVIDENCE – EXPLANATION

It is important that you construct your answer this way. If you just 'tell a story' in which you produce factual knowledge without explanation in relation to the question, you will not get high marks.

An example

Here is an example of a question asking you to produce not a story, but an explanation:

> (A) Why did North Korea attack South Korea on 25 June 1950?

The information to answer this question can be found in Section 1. The reasons you could include are:

- International factors – the increased confidence of Stalin and the triumph of Mao in China

- Personal factors – the character and personality of Kim Il Sung

- The Korean dimension – the intense rivalry for control of Korean nationalism and the process of Korean unification

- The military balance – the massive superiority of the North Korean Army by the summer of 1950.

As you plan, it is important to have a clear idea about the significance of these reasons. To do this, you must decide which factor was the most important. Your answer should convince the examiner that your opinion is correct.

Here is an example of a paragraph which could form part of your answer:

The most important reason why North Korean forces invaded the South in June 1950 is that Stalin had not only given Kim permission but made it possible for him to do so by rearming North Korea with the key equipment for such an attack. Stalin was feeling more confident in the power of the USSR after its acquisition of the atom bomb and the victory of the Communists in China. He felt that the Chinese could assist Kim if he came unstuck as a result of US intervention. However, Stalin thought US intervention was unlikely. As a result, Stalin and Kim were confident of a favourable outcome.

This is a good paragraph because:

- It begins with a clear statement which assesses a reason for the attack.

- It *prioritises* reasons by stating, in the opening sentence, that this was the key reason.

- The opening statement is backed up by evidence. It provides examples of the reasons why Stalin's confidence had grown.

Activity: Spot the mistake

Below are three paragraphs which attempt to explain why North Korea attacked South Korea. However, although the information in each paragraph is correct, there are mistakes in the way each paragraph is written. Your task is to spot the mistake in each paragraph and write one sentence of advice to the author of each paragraph explaining how they could do better.

Example 1

On 25 June, early in the morning, North Korean troops opened a heavy artillery attack on South Korea. Thousands of heavily armed troops rolled across the border, the 38th parallel. T-34 tanks played a major role in smashing through the lightly armed Republic of Korea forces. Seoul was soon occupied and South Korean forces were in headlong retreat, pushed steadily southwards towards the southern port of Pusan.

Example 2

Kim Il Sung had returned to Korea in 1945. He was a Korean patriot of long standing. He had fought the Japanese and spent much time in China and also in the Soviet Union, where he had become an officer in the Red Army. When he had been a young man he had changed his name to be like that of a historic Korean hero of the past. In 1945 he hoped to become a Korean Stalin and deliberately cultivated his Russian masters.

Example 3

Tension had been steadily rising in Korea between the north and south since 1948. There had been a series of tit-for-tat attacks by each side upon the other. Both wished to unite the whole country. North Korea wished for a communist country under Kim Il Sung, and Syngman Rhee hoped to create a West-leaning regime under his leadership. Neither side accepted the division. Syngman Rhee constantly pressed the USA for help and heavy equipment suitable for attack, which they refused.

Answers

Example 1 – this paragraph tells the story of the fighting but does not answer the question.

Example 2 – this paragraph contains lots of detailed information, some of which could be related to the question but in this form is not.

Example 3 – this paragraph is generally well written, but the final sentence goes off the point of the question.

Activity: Write your own paragraph

Now try writing a paragraph on one of the other reasons for the North Korean attack. The information you require is found throughout Section 1.

Remember to begin your paragraph by stating which factor you are going to address. Make sure that you support your answer with factual knowledge and evidence. Then conclude your paragraph by explaining how the evidence it provides answers the question.

You may find the following steps a useful guide:

1. First decide what point you are going to make. Make sure that the point is relevant to the question you have been asked. For example:

   ○ Tension had been growing between North and South Korea since 1948.

2. Decide which evidence you will use to support your point. But choose carefully – make sure that it is relevant and is linked directly to the point you are making.

3. Write your paragraph by:

   ○ Presenting your point

   ○ Backing your point up with evidence

   ○ Explaining how the evidence supports your point

   ○ Explaining how your point relates to the essay question.

Remember: POINT – EVIDENCE – EXPLANATION

Extension work

Here is an example of the style of question often used in the examination. It asks you to make a judgement about causes.

> (B) How far do you agree that the outbreak of a major conflict in Korea in 1950 was caused by Communist aggression?

If you were writing an essay-style answer to this question, you would be expected to select information which helps explain why the war occurred and to decide on the importance of Communist aggression compared with other factors, such as the personal rivalry of Kim and Syngman Rhee and American concerns. You may also wish to add factors of your own. Using the steps outlined above to help you, write a paragraph to form part of an essay in answer to the question.

Chapter 5   The origins of America's involvement in the Vietnam War, 1950–1960

Key questions

- What was the nature of Indo-China?
- In what ways was there a communist threat in South East Asia?
- Why did the USA give increasing aid to France in the years 1950–1954?
- Why was 1954 a key year in US involvement in South East Asia?
- How effective a ruler was Diem in South Vietnam in the years 1955–1960?

If the Korean War was the 'Forgotten War', then the Vietnam War is the 'Remembered War'. Iconic photographs abound, fixing the war in the memory of future generations: the burning Buddhist monk; the napalm-burned child, hopelessly fleeing its fate but captured forever with a camera shot; the Viet Cong soldier about to be executed. All these images became the common currency of the late-twentieth-century media. A series of popular films, such as *Apocalypse Now* (1979) and *Platoon* (1986), added to the range of images that the public carried in its shared memory. Few wars have elicited such debate as to its origin and resolution. The war divided America and still continues to do so. Why the USA became embroiled in an area of the world in which it had few interests and little traditional connection still excites wonder. Yet thousands of young Americans were to die there, ultimately to no avail.

Buddhist monk Thích Quàng Dúc's act of self-immolation in protest against the persecution of Buddhists by South Vietnam's Catholic Diem regime, 11 June 1963

Timeline

1945	Ho Chi Minh proclaims Vietnam's independence from the French; setting up of the Democratic Republic of Vietnam (DRV)
1946	Armed revolt against the returned French breaks out in Vietnam
1948	Communist insurgency in Malaya
1950	**June:** First US supplies sent to the French in Vietnam Communist China ships arms to the Viet Minh
1952	**November:** Eisenhower elected US president
1953	**January:** Dulles becomes US secretary of state
1954	**May:** Major French defeat at Dien Bien Phu **July:** Geneva Accords on the future of French Indo-China divides Vietnam at the 17th parallel **September:** SEATO (South East Asia Treaty Organisation) set up $2 billion sent in aid to South Vietnam from the USA
1955	Ngo Dinh Diem overthrows the monarchy and proclaims the Republic of Vietnam in the South with himself as president
1956	Diem reneges on all-Vietnam elections scheduled under the 1954 Geneva Accords DRV busy with internal problems in the North
1959	DRV Politburo decides to send substantial aid to communist opponents of Diem in the South; Second Vietnam War begins Geneva Accords break down in Laos
1960	Pathet Lao (communists) seem on the edge of victory in Laos, backed by USSR and DRV **November:** Kennedy elected US president

The nature of Indo-China

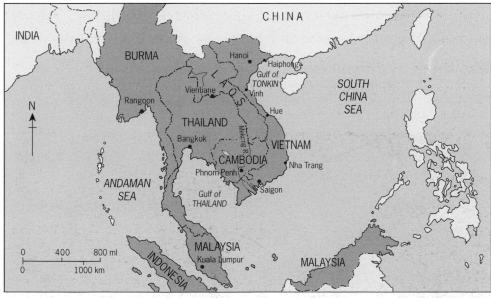

South East Asia

Indo-China, as its name indicates, is the area of Asia east of India and south of China. It is composed of six countries and the island city of Singapore at its southern tip. In the nineteenth century, Indo-China had been divided between the British and the French Empires, with an agreement reached to leave Thailand as a neutral barrier between the two. Laos, Cambodia and Vietnam were French-controlled and Burma and Malaya were controlled by the British. The whole area had been rapidly overrun by the Japanese

> ### Indo-China
>
> Indo-China and South East Asia are essentially the same area, containing the six countries of Burma, Cambodia, Laos, Malaya, Thailand and Vietnam. French Indo-China refers to Laos, Cambodia and Vietnam. (Note: Korea is not in South East Asia.)

in 1941–1942. White colonial supremacy suffered a devastating blow to its prestige. Britain abandoned Burma to independence after the war but returned to the rule of Malaya and Singapore. France sought to reimpose colonial rule on Laos, Cambodia and Vietnam but soon discovered that she faced an up-hill struggle. Vietnam was the key area which the French tried to regain.

Vietnam is a long, narrow country, which runs 1200 miles (1930 km) from north to south but varies in size from east to west, ranging from between 250 miles (400 km) and a mere 40 miles (64 km) at its very narrow waist in the centre. It lies in the tropics and much of the vegetation is tropical rainforest. Mountains, sometimes as high as 10,000 feet (3050 metres), separate Vietnam from China in the north and from Laos in the west. Its two great cities lie at opposite ends of the country – Hanoi in the north and, more than twice as large with a population in the 1950s of over 1.5 million, Saigon in the south. The country's chief export in the 1950s was rice. The total population of the country in the mid-1960s was roughly 35 million. French rule had also extended over Laos and Cambodia to the west of Vietnam. These two areas were much less important, with smaller populations mainly concentrated in the long valley of the Mekong River, which ran north–south. Laos, which is largely mountainous, had a population of only 2 million, and Cambodia, to the south, had a population of around 6.5 million. This tropical corner of Asia was about to become the scene of nearly 25 years of conflict, as the worldwide struggle between the USA and communism reached this area with devastating consequences.

Was there a communist threat in South East Asia?

The establishment of the Democratic Republic of Vietnam

The most important communist grouping was the Indo-Chinese Communist Party, founded in 1930. It was as much a nationalist party devoted to expelling the French as one promoting Soviet-style communism. Its leading light was **Ho Chi Minh**.

Ho Chi Minh, September 1969

In 1941 the Indo-Chinese Communist Party broadened its appeal by joining with other radical groups in the **Viet Minh**. The Viet Minh stressed national independence rather than Marxism, but was essentially a front organisation for the Communist Party, who pulled the real levers of power. During the next four years the Viet Minh fought the Japanese occupiers with American assistance. When the Japanese surrendered in 1945, Ho and the Viet Minh quickly proclaimed Vietnamese independence before the French could return. The Democratic Republic of Vietnam (DRV) was established in Hanoi with Ho as president.

Take note

As you read through this section, list the reasons why American help to the French increased between 1950 and 1954.
In what ways did it remain limited?

Ho Chi Minh

(1890–1969)

Ho was born in 1890 into a sufficiently wealthy family for him to be educated. His father was a committed anti-French nationalist. Ho left Vietnam in 1912 and travelled the world for the next 30 years. He learned English, French, Russian and Chinese, living in the USA, France, Russia and China. He became a communist in France but then studied 'revolutionary techniques' in Moscow. He worked in China for the Comintern agent Borodin.

The Viet Minh's influence in the south was less and the French began to reassert their authority there with British support. Ho hoped for US support or at least sympathy, and before the Cold War really developed this was not a vain hope. The USA declared its opposition to colonialism, gave the Philippines their independence and encouraged the Dutch to abandon Indonesia. Ho showed a willingness to negotiate but late in 1946 fighting broke out between French troops and the Viet Minh, which was to last for eight years.

US involvement in the French struggle against the Viet Minh

The triumph of Mao and the China Communists in 1949 transformed the situation and led the Truman administration to see Ho's forces as part of the same international grouping rather than an indigenous nationalist movement. There was little doubt that, as the struggle with France developed, the Viet Minh became more openly Marxist and with Mao's triumph began to receive aid from China. The USA encouraged the French to grant some degree of independence to the Vietnamese, which they did in 1949, making it easier for the USA, as an opponent of colonialism, to assist the French.

In February 1950 the USA recognised the French-backed government of the emperor **Bao Dai** as the legitimate government of Vietnam. On the last day of June, just after the Korean War had started, eight US transport planes touched down near Saigon and were rapidly handed over to the French air force. Later that year a US ship crammed with military hardware docked in the Saigon River. Massive US assistance was being made available to the French in their struggle with the Viet Minh. The USA had decided that the fighting in French Indo-China against Ho's nationalists was all part of the same struggle against Moscow and international communism.

In giving aid to France, the USA was also influenced by events in Europe. Here the confrontation with Soviet Russia over Berlin, culminating in the Berlin airlift of 1948–1949, had made America anxious for French support in NATO in confronting the USSR. By December 1953, the USA was providing France with 10,000 tons of equipment per month and the annual aid totalled $500 million. The USA was covering 75–80 per cent of the cost of the French struggle with the Viet Minh.

Domino theory

The justification for this vast expense was a belief that there was a 'communist threat' worldwide, orchestrated from Moscow. The new Republican vice president, Richard Nixon, visited Vietnam in December 1953 and, in a national television broadcast on his return, justified America's involvement:

> If Indo-China falls, Thailand is put in an almost impossible position. The same is true of Malaya with its rubber and tin. The same is true of Indonesia. If Indo-China goes under communist domination the whole of South East Asia will be threatened and that means that the economic and military security of Japan will inevitably be endangered also.

Here is what became known as the 'domino theory'. President Eisenhower

Viet Minh

This was a communist front organisation set up in 1941 by the Indo-Chinese Communist Party. It attempted to seize power in 1945 before French colonial rule could be reimposed. Its full name was Viet Nam Doc Lap Dong Minh Hoi.

Bao Dai

(1913–1997)

Emperor of Vietnam from 1926 to 1945. His power was nominal under French colonial rule and he was used briefly by the Japanese as a puppet ruler. He abdicated in August 1945 but became 'head of state' following an agreement with the French in 1950. He continued in this role until 1955 when he was removed by Diem. He retired to the South of France and the happy life of a playboy and died in 1997 at the age of 84.

Guerrilla warfare

Guerrilla literally means 'little war' in Spanish and use of the term 'guerrilla war' originated in the Peninsula War of 1808–1814, when Spanish partisans acting in small groups harassed the large French army occupying Spain. The essential principle of guerrilla warfare is to force a superior army which cannot be beaten in open battle to break up into small units to try to control a large area. The guerrillas then take on the small units. At Dien Bien Phu the Viet Minh abandoned guerrilla warfare and accepted the French challenge of a set-piece battle, which against expectation the Viet Minh won.

actually used the image of dominoes going over in a press conference in April 1954, but others in the US administration had frequently used the idea of a chain reaction of threat. The administration in the USA and the wider public had come to believe in the 'communist threat'. The fact that Mao was more a Chinese nationalist than a communist and that this was equally applicable to Ho Chi Minh, who was a Vietnamese nationalist first and a communist a poor second, was ignored. The more the USA seemed to confront international communism the more realistic the threat seemed to become. Mao was driven closer to Moscow because of his confrontation with the USA and likewise Ho was driven closer to Mao.

Ironically in 1951, the US War College, responsible for the training of senior officers, embarked on a study of US policy in South East Asia. Its conclusions were that Indo-China was of only secondary strategic importance to the USA and it was quite unsuitable as a place for the deployment of American troops. This point was fully appreciated by President Eisenhower, who having got the USA out of one unpopular war in Korea was anxious not to be landed in another.

French defeat at Dien Bien Phu

By 1954, French resolve to continue the struggle was weakening despite massive US help. The French, in a desperate throw against the Viet Minh decided to fortify a remote area in north Vietnam. It hoped this would cut supplies coming in from China and possibly force the Viet Minh **guerrillas** to come out and fight a traditional battle; the French believed the Viet Minh would surely lose in view of superior French fire power. The Viet Minh, under their talented General Giap, took up the challenge, dragging artillery through jungle and assembling a vast force against the 12,000 French soldiers, who relied entirely on air supplies. The result was the Battle of Dien Bien Phu, which ended in a crushing defeat for the French in early May 1954. Eisenhower came under intense pressure to send direct assistance but refused, always insisting that any American involvement must enjoy British support as well (he knew that this would not be forthcoming). Some of his advisers pressured him to use tactical nuclear strikes against Giap's forces. Eisenhower rejected such advice completely. France was defeated and a new chapter in Vietnam's history opened with the Geneva Conference in May 1954.

Communist insurgency in Malaya, 1948

There had also been another apparent communist threat in South East Asia, this time in the important British territory of Malaya. The situation here was complicated, not only by the merger of ideological conflict over communism with a struggle over colonialism, as in Vietnam, but inter-racial conflict. The chief opponents of British rule and the most active communists were drawn from the large Chinese minority in Malaya. They were, however, bitterly opposed by the native Malays, who feared Chinese domination in post-imperial freedom. The result was a twelve-year-long struggle, termed by the British, with appropriate understatement, as 'an emergency' not a war.

Conflict began in 1948. Attacks were waged on plantations and tin mines by the communist guerrillas, who tried to intimidate villages into supporting them. Opponents of the communists could be flayed and left tied up to have their bleeding bodies eaten alive by insects. The British Army, assisted by the Malay police, responded with counter-terror, dropping the decapitated heads of captured guerrillas back into the jungle to lower the morale of their comrades. The 'emergency' lasted 12 years but ended in the utter defeat of the communists and the establishment of a prosperous and capitalist Malaya, friendly to the West.

The presence of a communist threat in Malaya added to America's impression of a generalised communist conspiracy and gave support to those who upheld the domino theory. Communism had to be contained, it seemed to most people within the USA, or it would overrun Asia.

The Eisenhower administration and Vietnam

Take note

As you read through this section, make notes on how the Republican administration under Eisenhower differed in its policy from that of Truman's administration.

US president Dwight Eisenhower (left) and secretary of state John Foster Dulles (centre) with Ngo Dinh Diem (right), 1957.

The Republicans had won the presidential election of November 1952. On the surface they were more anti-communist than the Democrats and they had made much of the Democrats 'losing China' in the election (see page 7 of Chapter 1). There was a very strong 'China lobby' within the Party and the notorious red baiter, Joseph McCarthy, was a Republican senator. Dwight D. Eisenhower was in practice very moderate, with an approach to policy very similar to that of his predecessor, Truman. He was determined to continue the policy of 'containing' communism but this did not involve launching a crusade to roll back communism, despite the rhetoric used by some Republicans during the election.

The man Eisenhower appointed as secretary of state was John Foster Dulles, a devout Christian and hater of communism, who had talked of the desirability of freeing human beings from the tyranny of communist dictatorship. However, despite the words, Dulles was a sophisticated insider in terms of foreign policy, who had played an advisory role to Acheson in the previous administration. He understood the realities of foreign policy and the difference between public rhetoric and practical politics. Neither he nor Eisenhower was going to do anything which was likely to involve the USA in direct conflict with either the USSR or China. Communist subversion should be countered and clear lines maintained to contain its spread.

Eisenhower inherited an inflated defence budget (see Chapter 4, page 41) but he was anxious to prevent it getting out of hand. He appreciated the dangers of an uncontrolled arms race, which would not bring security. The USA already enjoyed nuclear superiority and Eisenhower was determined not to indulge the whims of every general and admiral pressing for more and more military hardware. He therefore cut spending with the ending of the Korean War in 1953 and was determined not to get into another Asian war if it could possibly be avoided. Eisenhower believed that a balanced budget and a prosperous America was the best answer to the communist threat. The key solution to holding the line in South East Asia was a prosperous, independent but non-communist Vietnam, backed up by an international organisation to guard against future subversion.

The Geneva Conference and Accords, May–July 1954

The USA was not to get everything it desired. Half of Vietnam was to be lost to communism, but half a cake is better than none and in the aftermath of the French defeat at Dien Bien Phu it looked as though the Viet Minh would sweep all before it. The French were increasingly unwilling to continue the struggle and the British refused to intervene. The USA lacked the troops or the will for direct intervention. Ho appreciated his strong position and it took serious pressure from the Chinese and Russians to persuade him to compromise.

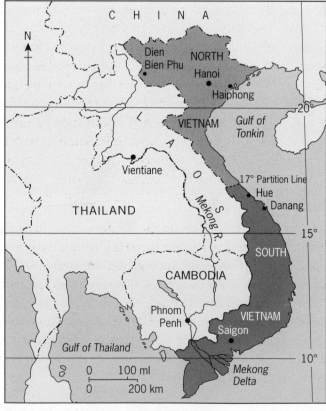

The division of Vietnam at the 17th parallel

> **Take note**
>
> As you read through this section, make notes on why the DRV was so reluctant to sign the Geneva Accords.

The conference in Geneva, Switzerland, was jointly chaired by Britain and the USSR, both anxious to moderate the tensions of the Cold War. The Chinese feared direct US intervention in Vietnam and wanted the conflict ended. The USA was not directly involved in the conference and refused to recognise the Chinese delegation as legitimate, so sent only observers but still exercised influence behind the scenes. A change in the government in France in June enabled a deal to be made between the new French government and the Chinese premier, **Zhou Enlai**. Ho reluctantly accepted what his Chinese sponsor agreed. The result was the **Geneva Accords**.

> **Geneva Accords**
>
> These ended the first Vietnam War (between France and the Viet Minh) and laid the basis for the second. Vietnam was to be divided at the 17th parallel, with the north controlled by the Viet Minh and the south by Bao Dai and the French. The French were to withdraw from the north and the Viet Minh from the south. Laos and Cambodia were to be independent and neutral. There were to be elections held in 1956 to secure the reunification of Vietnam. There were to be no foreign troops in any of the four territories.

The US response to the Geneva Accords: increased involvement in Vietnam

The USA did not see the conference as a success, merely the best that could be salvaged. They were suspicious of the elections to secure the reunification of Vietnam, promised for 1956, as it was assumed by all that Ho would win these. He completely controlled the population in North Vietnam, which formed a slight majority of the population of all of Vietnam. The answer to the USA seemed to be to build up South Vietnam, free from the French and the taint of colonialism, as an effective barrier. There was a view in the State Department that an opportunity had been missed in China to secure the south of the country, free from communist control, if only Chiang Kai-shek (Jiang Jieshi) had been more realistic. In Korea, division seemed to have worked. What was needed was a suitable strong man in South Vietnam, and the USA, after some doubts, hit upon **Ngo Dinh Diem**. He was very much backed by the CIA and had powerful friends in Washington, among them the young Democratic senator John F. Kennedy, a fellow Roman Catholic.

The USA, therefore, set about creating a viable South Vietnamese state. The French first withdrew from the North, as agreed at Geneva, and then pulled out of the South in 1955, leaving a poorly officered native force, which would be no match for the Viet Minh. Diem was appointed prime minister by Bao Dai in June 1954 and the USA agreed to extend massive aid to the government of South Vietnam at the end of September 1954. The agency for much of this was **MAAG** (Military Assistance Advisory Group), which from 1955 became heavily involved in training the ARVN (Army of the Republic of Vietnam).

Zhou Enlai

(1898–1975)

A leading figure in the Chinese Communist Party who became both premier and foreign minister of the People's Republic of China. He was considered to be a skilled and able diplomat and arguably one of the supreme negotiators of the twentieth century. Possibly his greatest challenge was during the Cultural Revolution in China (1966–1969) when he worked to preserve national unity and the survival of the government against the forces of anarchy.

Ngo Dinh Diem

(1901–1963)

A wealthy Vietnamese Catholic and nationalist. He was personally not corrupt but very distrustful of all but his own family. He tended to favour Catholics, who were a minority in a largely Buddhist country and he had little rapport with the peasant masses.

MAAG

The Military Assistance Advisory Group played a major part in training the South Vietnamese Army (Army of the Republic of Vietnam, or ARVN) from 1955 to 1964. It was headed by a US general and, until 1960, had a nominal total of 342 advisers. This was the maximum of foreign military personnel allowed by the Geneva Accords.

As the French withdrew, the US moved in to become the essential support to the southern state. There were some doubts as to whether Diem was suitable but his ruthless crushing of the criminal Binh Xuyen organisation, which controlled much of the vice in Saigon and supplied funds to Emperor Bao Dai, convinced many doubters. Diem also showed political skill in doing deals with two powerful religious sects who controlled militias in the south, and by April 1955 Dulles' and Eisenhower's doubts about Diem had been relieved if not entirely removed.

In the USA, the American Friends of Vietnam association was established to press for support for Diem. It included some fire-eating anti-communists but also liberal Democrats like Senators John Kennedy and Mike Mansfield. Diem consolidated his hold on power by securing the abdication of Bao Dai and his own appointment as president of the new Republic of Vietnam in October 1955. This seemed to mark a clean break from the colonial past. The regime was also strengthened by the mass emigration from the North Vietnamese state of hundreds of thousands of Catholic Vietnamese, encouraged both by their priests and CIA-orchestrated propaganda. There was far less movement from the South as Viet Minh supporters assumed that in 1956 the two halves would be reunited under Ho's government.

Failure of the 1956 elections

When 1956 arrived and, according to the Geneva Accords, elections for the reunification of Vietnam were due, Diem refused to discuss with the DRV arrangements for the elections, which simply failed to take place. A process of repression of dissidents and Viet Minh supporters in the South followed, carried out by Diem's brother Ngo Dinh Nhu as head of the security forces. Thousands were arrested and killed. The failure to hold elections was resented in North Vietnam but Ho and the government had their own hands full establishing a totalitarian hold on the country and carrying through Soviet-style land reform (which involved a similar degree of repression as was being dosed out in the South). Two dictatorships were being established under cover of the Cold War. The USA was well aware of the repression in the South but contented itself with the view that this was better than if there were a communist government in the South too, and that eventually some sort of liberal regime would emerge. Diem's government was simply seen as the only regime available as an alternative to Viet Minh victory.

SEATO

In another important respect, 1954 marked a significant stage in American involvement in South East Asia. In September 1954, Dulles succeeded in establishing the South East Asia Treaty Organisation (SEATO). It was signed in Manila, and Australia, New Zealand, France, Britain, Pakistan, the Philippines, Thailand and the USA joined. The ex-states of French Indo-China were forbidden to join such a pact under the Geneva Accords, but SEATO guaranteed their security. The aim of the pact was mutual defence and it was meant to assist in the containment of communism in the region.

Take note

Look at the map on page 47 and find as many of these countries as you can.

In 1956, Diem further broke the Accords by joining SEATO as an associate member. On the surface the pact looked to have established an anti-communist alliance like NATO (North Atlantic Treaty Organisation) in Europe, but in reality SEATO was less binding.

Nevertheless, it appeared that containment had been applied in South East Asia, and, until 1959, it appeared to be working. The British had largely defeated the communist insurgency in Malaya. In South Vietnam it did appear that a viable South Vietnamese state had been achieved, even if Diem's regime was hardly a showcase for Western democracy. The North Vietnamese state appeared to have abstained from effective interference in the South. This was to change in 1959–1960 and real problems were to confront the new presidential administration of John F. Kennedy.

Activity: Getting to grips with South East Asia

1. List all the individuals mentioned in this chapter and identify their nationality, political beliefs and importance in shaping events in South East Asia.

2. Look carefully at the map of the region and make sure that you know the position of each country. Note the positions of Saigon and Hanoi in Vietnam and Phnom Penh in Cambodia.

3. Find satellite images from the internet (e.g. Google Earth) to get a sense of what Vietnam is like.

Taking it further

Try to understand why the French lost in 1954 by carrying out a detailed study of the Battle of Dien Bien Phu. Three very different viewpoints of the battle are contained in the following books:

- *Hell in a Very Small Place: the Siege of Dien Bien Phu* (1966) by B. Fall
- *Dien Bien Phu* (2000) by Vo Nguyen Giap
- *End of a War: Indochina, 1954* (1969) by J. Lacouture.

Skills Builder 2: Planning answers to questions on causation and change

Questions on causation

In the AS examination you may be asked questions on causation – questions about what caused historical events to take place.

Some questions may ask you to explain why something happened. For example:

> (A) Why did Eisenhower decide to intervene in South East Asia in the 1950s?

Other questions on causation will ask you to assess the importance of one cause of an event in relation to other causes. These often begin with 'How far' or 'To what extent'. Here is an example:

> (B) How far do you agree that the 'domino theory' explains US intervention in South East Asia in the 1950s?

Planning your answer

Before you write your essay you need to make a plan. In the exam you will have to do this very quickly! The first thing to do is to identify the key points you will make in your answer. Let's look at some examples.

When planning an answer to Question (A) you need to note down reasons why the USA intervened in Vietnam. You can do this in the form of a list or a concept map.

When planning an answer to Question (B) you need to think about the importance of each reason. You could:

- Write a list of all the reasons then number them in order of importance.

- Draw a concept map with 'US intervention' at the centre, and put the most important reasons near the middle and the least important reasons further away.

It is much easier to assess the importance of one factor when you have a list of all the relevant factors in front of you!

The information you require for these answers can be found in Chapter 5. Go to Chapter 5 and identify the reasons why Eisenhower intervened.

Linking the causes

Once you have identified the relevant information and organised it, it is important to highlight links between the reasons.

In making your plan, try grouping reasons together which have links. If you have produced a list of reasons, you may want to rearrange the points where you can identify clear links between them. If you have drawn a concept map, you could draw arrows between the linked points.

Writing your answer

For Question (A) above, you could write a paragraph on each cause. Alternatively, you might want to start with what you think is the most important cause and then deal with the other causes.

For Question (B) above, it is essential that you refer to the relative importance of different causes, focusing particularly on the role of the 'domino theory'. Remember to answer the question! You might want to deal with the domino theory first and then assess the importance of other points explaining US involvement in Vietnam. Make sure you write a separate paragraph for each reason that you identify.

Questions about change

These questions will require you to explain how far a specified factor changed during a historical period.

Examples of this type of question would be:

> (C) How far did the role of the USA in South East Asia change in the years 1950–1963?

> (D) How far did the role of the USA in South East Asia increase in the years 1950–1963?

Planning your answer

When you plan, organise your material in a way that will help you to answer the question.

For instance, for Question (C) you could begin by listing two or three ways in which the role of the USA changed. Having done that, you could list two or three ways in which the role of the USA remained limited. Alternatively, you could arrange this information on one or two concept maps. Remember that your answer needs to be balanced. Therefore, it should provide points for and against change.

Each of these points will form the basis for one paragraph in your answer. In the last Skills Builder section, you considered the importance of providing specific examples to support your points. Don't forget this!

When you plan, there is no need to organise your material in a chronological way. This may encourage the writing of descriptive or narrative-style answers. Such answers may contain lots of accurate and relevant historical information, but may not be directly focused on the question.

Writing your answer

In Questions (C) and (D) you are asked 'how far' in relation to changes. So in your final paragraph, the conclusion, you will be expected to make a *judgement*. Based on the historical evidence you have presented in your answer, you should decide, and state, whether you believe the situation mainly changed or mainly stayed the same.

Activity: how much have you learned?

Here are some examples of questions which deal with causation and change. First, identify the causation questions and give a reason to support your choice. Then identify the questions which deal with change and give a reason for your choice. Finally, choose one 'causation' question and one 'change' question and produce a plan for each, showing how you would organise your answer.

(E) How far was increasing aggression on the part of North Vietnam the main cause of increasing US intervention in South Vietnam?

(F) How far did the degree of US intervention in South East Asia under President Kennedy (1961–1963) differ from that under President Johnson (1963–1968)?

(G) To what extent was growing opposition in the USA the reason for President Nixon's decision to withdraw ground forces from Vietnam?

(H) In what ways did the aims of the USA change during the Korean War?

Chapter 6   The Kennedy years, 1960–1963

Key questions

- What legacy in Vietnam did Kennedy inherit from Eisenhower?
- In what ways and why did the Kennedy administration increase US involvement in South East Asia?
- Why was Diem removed in 1963?

The new president who succeeded Eisenhower seemed to have everything: youth, good looks, brains and money in abundance. He charmed the media then and has since. Yet he advanced significantly into the Vietnam quagmire, with less caution than his elderly Republican predecessor had shown. Kennedy appeared youthful when contrasted with Eisenhower and had an appealing self-confidence and a firm belief in the power of America to 'pay any price, bear any burden ... to assure the survival and success of liberty'.

Timeline

1959	Renewed fighting in Laos Democratic Republic of Vietnam (DRV) increased support to communist rebels in South Vietnam
1960	**November:** Kennedy elected US president Attempted coup against Diem by South Vietnamese Army units **December:** National Liberation Front (NLF) set up to unite opponents of Diem
1961	Growing tension over Berlin **May:** Vice President Johnson returns from Vietnam visit **October:** Rostow–Taylor mission to South Vietnam **December:** Approximately 3200 US military personnel stationed in South Vietnam
1962	**February:** Military Assistance Command Vietnam (MACV) established **July:** Geneva Accords on Laos **October:** Cuban Missile Crisis **December:** Approximately 11,300 US military personnel stationed in South Vietnam
1963	**January:** Battle of Ap Bac **May:** Growing crisis with Buddhist majority in South Vietnam **November:** Diem removed from power and murdered Kennedy assassinated; Johnson becomes president. Approximately 16,300 US military personnel stationed in South Vietnam

Take note

List the problems in Indo-China facing the incoming US administration.

Why did Kennedy feel that he could not ignore Indo-China?

Growing problems in Indo-China, 1959–1960

By 1960, the last year of the Eisenhower presidency, containment in South East Asia seemed under renewed challenge. This was perhaps most serious in the under-populated Kingdom of Laos. The North Vietnamese had never really withdrawn from this region and the Pathet Lao, the native communist organisation, heavily supported by the North Vietnamese, appeared to be on the point of dominating the whole country. In other words, another domino, if a small one, was about to fall.

Trouble was also developing in South Vietnam, although initially it was not seen to be as pressing as the communist threat in Laos. In the course of 1959, the Politburo in Hanoi, the governing body of North Vietnam, appears to have decided to step up aid to communist supporters in South Vietnam, who were under pressure from the Diem regime. Many of those who had left South Vietnam in 1954 were sent back to encourage and help the insurgency against Diem. Furthermore, the North Vietnamese government reactivated the so-called Ho Chi Minh Trail along the Laos and Cambodian border as a means of supplying arms to the fighters in South Vietnam. This made the situation in Laos all the more crucial. In December 1960, a month before Eisenhower handed over to Kennedy, an anti-Diem coalition was formed in South Vietnam, calling itself the **National Liberation Front (NLF)**.

The growing unpopularity of the Diem regime was an essential part of the problem. To some writers he appears simply as a US **stooge**, but in reality he was anything but. Stubborn, arrogant and distrustful of all but his family, he often failed to take proffered advice from the American representatives in Vietnam and treated them to interminable lectures on how right he was. Power remained simply with his relatives, a situation ably expressed by his sister-in-law, Madame Nhu: 'All power is lovely. Absolute power is absolutely lovely.'

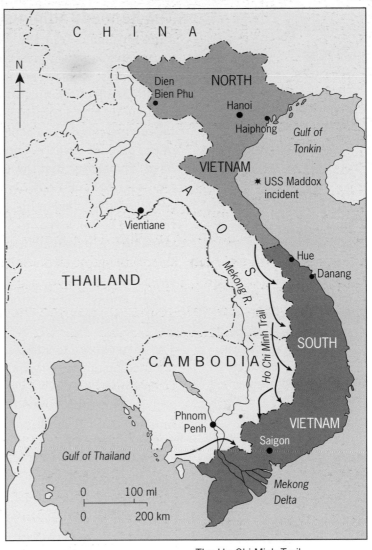

The Ho Chi Minh Trail

Reforms under Diem came too little and too late. He embarked on a policy of 'Agrovilles', uprooting peasants from their villages and herding them into new rural towns where in theory they could enjoy the benefits of education and welfare. In reality, such moves were resented, as peasants had to leave their traditional lands and the graves of their parents and ancestors (Vietnam had a culture which felt a deep reverence for past family members). The Buddhist majority of the population were treated with contempt and the Catholic minority openly favoured. In 1959, Diem had dedicated the Republic of Vietnam to the Virgin Mary, not the most tactful or politically sensitive of gestures.

In November 1960, the month Kennedy was elected president, two colonels in the Army of the Republic of Vietnam (ARVN) attacked the presidential palace with a group of soldiers. Diem was lucky to survive. The revolt only increased his distrust of all but his closest associates and made him less likely to take US advice.

National Liberation Front (NLF)

This was a communist-dominated organisation; its critics referred to it as a 'communist front'. Its chairman was a Saigon lawyer opposed to Diem but not himself a communist. Sympathisers with the rebels used the name NLF, but opponents called them the Viet Cong, which is short for *công sán Viêt Nam* (meaning Vietnamese communist).

Robert McNamara

(Born 1916)

He was a major influence on the conduct of the Vietnam War under both Kennedy and Johnson while he served as Secretary of Defense from 1961 to 1968. He supported the escalation of the conflict in Vietnam but began to have doubts by 1966. The film made around his career, *The Fog of War* (2003), is an excellent accessory to this course.

Take note

As you read through this section, think about the measures adopted by the Kennedy administration to deal with the increased communist threat. Make a concept map giving each bullet point a label of no more than three words. Better still, try to do it in one.

Vietnam quagmire

An important metaphor used by some commentators and historians to explain US involvement in South Vietnam, i.e. the USA had waded almost unknowingly into a muddy swamp from which it could not extricate itself.

The Kennedy administration

John Fitzgerald Kennedy's arrival in the White House returned the Democrats to power after Eisenhower's presidency. It had been a knife-edge contest with the Republican Richard Nixon, who had a reputation as a hardline anti-communist. Kennedy had played up his own anti-communist credentials in the campaign and accused the Eisenhower administration of neglecting certain key aspects of defence. The Democrats were well aware of the damage that the criticism that they were soft on communism could have. The charge that the Democrats had 'lost China' was still bandied about (see page 51) and Kennedy was determined that no similar accusations were going to be levelled at his administration. Defence spending was increased from $40 billion a year to $56 billion. The number of nuclear delivery vehicles was massively increased and there was a new emphasis on meeting the challenge of revolutionary subversive movements through the use of specially trained forces. These became the elite US Special Forces – the 'Green Berets' (after Kennedy authorised them to wear a green beret as a mark of distinction).

The man chosen to supervise the big increase in defence spending was a talented business 'whiz kid', **Robert McNamara.** He, like many of the new faces around Kennedy, was among the 'brightest and the best' of US business and academic life. It was not 'fuddy-duddy' **conservatives** who took the USA into Vietnam, but well-intentioned **liberal intellectuals**, anxious to defend freedom and promote a better world.

Conservatives

In the USA, the term 'conservative' is usually associated with the Republican Party and supporters of 'old fashioned values' such as religion, family and patriotism – but not if it was too expensive, as they also supported cheap government and low taxes. Many conservatives in the 1950s disliked the new world role taken on by the USA and wanted to return to isolation as in the nineteenth century.

Liberal intellectuals

In the USA, 'liberal' tends to be used where 'left wing' might be used in Britain. Liberals are likely to be Democrat Party supporters.

Why did the Kennedy administration increase US involvement in Vietnam?

In understanding why the Kennedy administration took the USA further into the '**Vietnam quagmire**', it is important to grasp some of its basic assumptions.

● Firstly, everything was set in a Cold War context. The USA was perceived to be locked in a worldwide conflict with the Soviet Union in which revolutionary subversion was the key chosen Soviet weapon. Ho Chi Minh had received training in Moscow and his whole regime in North Vietnam could not be conceived of as separate from the worldwide communist conspiracy to subvert Western capitalism and liberal values.

- The second great influence on the Kennedy generation was the curse of appeasement. It seemed to most who had come through the Second World War that the great mistake made before the war was not standing up to Hitler in time. Kennedy as a young and aspiring politician had written *While England Slept* (1940). He drew attention to the failures in British pre-war policy. It appeared that the only way to deal with dictators, whether German, Russian, Chinese or North Vietnamese, was to stand up to them.

- Thirdly, there was an enormous self-confidence in American economic and military power. The USA was not Britain in the 1930s, struggling with serious economic problems during the Depression. America was a 'can do' country, and in the Second World War she had shown this to the benefit of humanity. American prestige could not be sacrificed nor did it need to be.

- Finally, American politicians were acutely aware of the power of US anti-communist sentiment, which could break a politician (as McCarthy had so ably shown in the early 1950s). Democracy in the USA tended to produce simplifications of the world situation. Cold calculations of US interest and cost–benefit analyses of whether it was worth getting involved in Vietnam did not tend to play as well as high-sounding platitudes about crusading for freedom. It was easier for the average American voter to see Ho Chi Minh as the little devil in the service of the greater devils in Beijing and Moscow than as a sincere Vietnamese nationalist who happened to be a communist as well.

Thus, for a variety of reasons and assumptions there was little challenge to the policy of confronting the Viet Cong. Hardly anyone around the president dissented from the policy. Greater involvement in the affairs of South Vietnam was not due to a military conspiracy or the interests of the **military–industrial complex**, but a shared belief that communism had to be contained and the USA had the power to do this.

The growing commitment, 1961–1962

There were less than 1000 US military personnel in South Vietnam when Eisenhower handed over to Kennedy in January 1960, but even this number was in breach of the 1954 agreements, which stated that there were to be no foreign troops in Vietnam. The American military presence was therefore concealed by various deceptive devices. The policy of surreptitious intervention was stepped up in March 1961 when US planes were ordered to destroy any hostile aircraft over South Vietnam. However, any resulting damage to US planes was to be described by MAAG (Military Assistance Advisory Group) as 'accidental' not as a result of combat.

American policy under Kennedy was set out in a National Security Action Memorandum in May 1961 (NSAM 52). It committed the US 'to prevent communist domination … and to initiate, on an accelerated basis, a series of mutually supporting actions of a military, political, economic, psychological and covert character'. Here was the blueprint for escalation.

Military–industrial complex

This was a phrase used by Eisenhower in a speech of 17 January 1961, warning against the development and influence of powerful self-interest groups in the defence industries and the armed forces. Eisenhower feared that such groups might twist US policy to suit their interests and not those of the American people, for example by encouraging an unnecessarily high defence budget, not because the USA required it, but to boost their company profits. The concept became a favourite one among some extreme critics of the Vietnam War.

Take note

As you read through this section, consider to what extent the USA's involvement in South East Asia had increased by 1962.

Lyndon B. Johnson

(1908–1973)

A leading Democratic politician from Texas. Before becoming vice president in 1961 he was leader of the Democrats in the Senate. His influence as vice president was not great but events late in 1963 unexpectedly transformed the situation and led to him becoming president.

A series of missions left for Saigon to find out what was necessary. Vice President **Johnson** went in May and returned convinced that there was only Diem to prevent a communist takeover. Johnson referred to him as 'the Winston Churchill of South East Asia'. Money was promised and, later, US support in the way of training and cash to expand the ARVN. In 1961, military aid rose from $220 million to $262 million.

Many advisers around Kennedy began to press for the deployment of US troops. McGeorge Bundy, Kennedy's special assistant for national security affairs, and his deputy, Walt Rostow, felt that a tougher line was needed. Kennedy was reluctant and sent out further fact-finding missions, the most important being one under General Maxwell Taylor and Rostow in October. Taylor recommended a massive increase in aid as being necessary, including the deployment of some US troops. Most of Kennedy's key advisers gave support to Taylor. Eventually Kennedy agreed to step up intervention but not to include ground combat troops. Nevertheless, the number of trainers was to increase dramatically and helicopters and air support would be provided, flown by US personnel.

As US involvement in Vietnam increased in 1962, there were inevitable questions from the press as to the extent of America's role in the region, which the administration tried to play down. Officially the USA were there in support, but as Averell Harriman, the new assistant secretary of state, pointed out, it often appeared that the USA was assuming responsibility for the war against the Viet Cong. Operations were led and initiated by US advisers and often used English code names.

Compromise in Laos

In the much smaller country of Laos, Kennedy displayed more caution. It bordered China and he did not wish to repeat MacArthur's mistakes in Korea and bring the Chinese directly into confrontation with the USA. Negotiations in Geneva began in 1961 and a deal largely brokered between the USSR and the USA led to a temporary settlement. These Geneva Accords of 1962 established a neutral Laos and US military advisers were withdrawn. However, DRV forces did not withdraw as they promised and Laos remained vital as part of the chain of communication between North and South Vietnam. The so-called Ho Chi Minh Trail continued to operate and the USA's unwillingness to impede it effectively was to be a major handicap to winning the war in the South.

Take note

As you read through this section, list the reasons for the downfall of Diem. Why had the USA first accepted and supported him but in 1963 abandoned him?

The downfall of Diem, 1963

A constant worry with the USA was the character of Diem and his regime. The brutality of his rule meant that he was clearly not an ideal figurehead for resistance to communism in the name of democracy. Furthermore, he was increasingly seen as incompetent in his supervision of the South Vietnamese Army (ARVN). He appeared over-anxious to minimise casualties among his troops at the expense of effective action. He was hypersensitive to criticism and ever ready to take offence. In 1962 he expelled various American journalists from NBC, CBS and *Newsweek* for reporting his defects, in particular his tendency to talk at length and say nothing of importance. Some had criticised the **strategic hamlets** programme which had been adopted with the intention of lessening support for the Viet Cong. Basically Diem had little sense of what a Western democratic politician had to put up with in terms of criticism.

In January 1963, the weaknesses of the Army of the Republic of Vietnam (ARNV) were glaringly displayed in what became known as the Battle of Ap Bac. Outnumbered four to one, a Viet Cong battalion out-fought an ARVN force despite superior fire power and hardware. The US adviser attached to the army was appalled and wrote a report accusing ARVN officers of cowardice. There was a growing sense of frustration from the US embassy in Saigon downwards to officers like Lieutenant Colonel Vann, who wrote the report on Ap Bac.

It was the Diem regime's confrontation with the Buddhist majority that was to prove the final straw. This began in May 1963 when Diem's government prohibited the use of Buddhist religious flags. Demonstrations followed, and when protestors defied the ban to celebrate the annual Buddhist festival of Wesak, government forces fired on the crowd killing nine people. In response to the deaths, on 11 June, Thích Quàng Dúc, a senior Buddhist monk, doused himself in petrol and, while sitting calmly, burned himself to death. Quàng Dúc's suicide by fire attracted the world press. Further suicides followed and Diem's sister-in-law, Madame Nhu, in her typically 'sensitive' fashion, heightened the disgust worldwide by reference to 'a barbecued monk'. Diem refused all US advice to compromise and proclaimed martial law with widespread arrests. Some in the South Vietnamese army (ARNV) began to plan a **coup**, and although the USA did not instigate it there was an increasingly widely held view that Diem's departure would be a good thing for the fight against communism.

The coup came in early November. Despite knowledge of it, the CIA and US authorities in Saigon chose not to warn Diem. He was deposed and murdered along with his hated younger brother. Kennedy was horrified by the murder although he had accepted the inevitability of Diem's removal. Kennedy himself died later the same month, the victim of an assassin's bullet.

The Kennedy legacy

Johnson, Kennedy's successor, inherited a very difficult situation in South Vietnam. The numbers of US advisers had been increased massively to over 16,000 and special forces had been deployed; yet still the government of South Vietnam was tottering. After all this increased involvement and expenditure, withdrawal and the acceptance of a communist victory would be more difficult than it would have been under Eisenhower. Kennedy's tacit approval of the coup against Diem further increased the US commitment to an independent South Vietnam.

Strategic hamlets

This scheme began in some areas in 1961. It aimed to deprive the Viet Cong of rural support by putting peasants into fortified and protected villages where they could not be intimidated. It was modelled on the scheme developed in Malaya by the British, where it had been successful in the long-run. In South Vietnam it was less successful and suffered from the same defects as Diem's Agrovilles (see page 59).

Glossary:
Coup

A usually violent overthrow of an existing government and seizure of power, normally carried out by the army.

Hawks and doves

This phrase was used to describe the differing approaches to the war in Vietnam. Hawks wanted to pursue the war with enthusiasm to force the Democratic Republic of Vietnam to accept the South. McNamara and Bundy were seen as hawks but McNamara turned 'dovish' in 1967. The arch hawk was the head of the air force, General Curtis Le May. Doves wanted to halt the build-up and seek some compromise solution, but hardly any wanted simply to pull out.

Historians have argued ever since as to what Kennedy would have done, had he lived. Some critics of Johnson, his successor, have argued that Kennedy intended to withdraw; they like to draw attention to the statement he made in 1963 that it should be possible to withdraw 1000 advisers shortly and to wind down the whole US commitment by 1965. In the 1992 film, *JFK*, the director Oliver Stone even pushed the ludicrous and utterly unsubstantiated view that Kennedy was actually assassinated to make possible a greater involvement in Vietnam. In reality, Kennedy appears to have been unclear himself what it was necessary to do. He had repeatedly shown a deep reluctance to commit US ground troops and talked the day before he died of setting up a study group to examine every option, 'including how to get out of there'. Nevertheless, he had stated in public, on many occasions, his commitment to keeping South Vietnam out of communist control. His policy options changed with the degree of optimism regarding the situation in South Vietnam. Optimistic reports of success against the Viet Cong brought forth talk of the possibility of withdrawal; pessimism produced talk of the need to stick it out. In one of his last press conferences he stated: 'In my opinion, for us to withdraw from that effort, would mean a collapse not only of South Vietnam but South East Asia, so we are going to stay there'.

Activity: Hawks versus doves

Taking it further

For a critical view of US policy in the 1950s but forming an essential background to the legacy Kennedy inherited, read Graham Greene's novel of 1955, *The Quiet American* (or watch the film version of it).

Class debate

Divide into four groups:

A – Argue that Eisenhower was essentially ignorant when it came to Vietnam

B – Argue that Eisenhower was essentially idealistic when it came to Vietnam.

C – Argue that JFK was essentially ignorant when it came to Vietnam.

D – Argue that JFK was essentially idealistic when it came to Vietnam.

Working together as a group, imagine you are part of Kennedy's advisory team.

- Half of the group should take the line of the Hawks, pressing for greater action against the communists and for the deployment of troops. Think out what steps you would urge the president to take and what argument can be deployed in favour of such action. Hawks included at this time Kennedy's brother Robert, McGeorge Bundy and Rostow (as stated above) and Maxwell Taylor, chairman of the Joint Chiefs of Staff from 1962.

- Half of the group should play the part of the Doves, who included Dean Rusk at the State Department and Mike Mansfield, Senate majority leader, who opposed the deployment of troops. Think out what arguments can be put forward against sending troops to Vietnam.

Further background information on the hawks and the doves can be found in Chapter 13 of Robert Dallek's biography of Kennedy, *An Unfinished Life: John F. Kennedy, 1917–1963*, published in 2003.

Chapter 7 The Johnson years, 1963–1967

Key questions

- What were Johnson's policy options?
- Why was US involvement in Vietnam increased so markedly?
- What was achieved by the end of 1967?

Lyndon B. Johnson, the American president forever associated with the Vietnam War, was also its most prominent victim. It was not a war that he desired in any way. He, unlike Kennedy, was not primarily interested in foreign policy. He was experienced in manipulating Congress and an old-style Democrat, anxious to promote what he called the 'Great Society'. This involved reforms in the USA such as civil rights for black Americans and Medicare (free medical treatment) for the poor. He was not as closely associated as JFK with the anti-communism of McCarthy, nor had he been, like Kennedy, a member of the American Friends of Vietnam. He aimed to cut defence spending to make way for domestic reforms and this is what he did in his first year in office. Yet he inherited a situation in Vietnam, which trapped him and drove him unwillingly into a series of decisions for which his reputation has suffered ever since. The man of peace and reform became the man held responsible for the deaths of Vietnamese children and ever increasing numbers of young US troops.

Timeline

1963	**November:** Kennedy assassinated **December:** North Vietnam decides to intensify the war in the South
1964	**January:** Johnson approves covert operations against North Vietnam; coup in Saigon **August:** Gulf of Tonkin incidents; Tonkin Gulf Resolution passed by Congress **November:** Johnson beats Goldwater with a landslide **December:** Approximately 23,300 US military personnel in South Vietnam
1965	**February:** Johnson approves Operation Rolling Thunder **March:** Two US Marine battalions deployed to guard US air bases **May:** First large anti-war demonstration in Washington **June:** General Westmoreland empowered to commit US ground forces to combat **November:** Battle of Ia Drang Valley, the first major battle between US forces and North Vietnamese Army **December:** Approximately 184,300 US military personnel in South Vietnam
1966	**January:** US resumes bombing of North Vietnam **December:** Approximately 385,300 US military personnel in South Vietnam
1967	**February:** US mines some harbours and rivers in Democratic Republic of Vietnam **June:** Soviet freighter hit by US bombs **September:** Nguyen Van Thieu elected President of Republic of Vietnam **October:** Anti-war demonstration in Washington turns violent **December:** Approximately 485,600 US military personnel in South Vietnam

Lyndon Baines Johnson, president of the United States from 1963–1969

Take note

As you read through this section, identify the different factors forcing Johnson to intervene in South Vietnam with more men and resources.

Nguyen Van Thieu

(1923–2001)

General in the South Vietnamese Army, who provided many of the troops for the coup that overthrew Diem in 1963. He was selected by other leading generals and approved of by the USA to run in the presidential election of 1967. He became the effective ruler until 1975, always opposed to any compromise with the NLF and communists. He ended as an exile in the USA and died in 2001.

Cuban Missile Crisis

This was one of the key moments of danger during the Cold War, when the tension between the USA and USSR looked likely to boil up into military conflict. The Soviet Union attempted to place nuclear armed missiles in Cuba aimed at the USA. After a period of extreme tension, the Russians agreed to withdraw the missiles.

The predicament of Lyndon Baines Johnson

LBJ, as the new president was known, inherited his foreign policy advisers, but most importantly he inherited a situation in South Vietnam to which there was no easy solution. The 1963 coup against Diem, to which the Kennedy regime had assented, increased the sense of obligation to South Vietnam and increased the hope of a more effective resistance to communist pressure. In effect it increased political instability, and a series of coups followed until eventually, in 1967, **Nguyen Van Thieu** emerged as the undisputed leader. In the meantime, the Viet Cong stepped up their pressure, helped substantially by North Vietnam's decision in 1963 to intensify the conflict by supplying increasing support to the Viet Cong in the form of men and hardware. From late 1964, actual regiments of North Vietnamese soldiers began to operate in the South, particularly near the demilitarised zone and the Laos and Cambodian borders. It seemed that unless increased US involvement took place, South Vietnam would fall, despite the 16,000 advisers placed there by Kennedy and the growing US air power.

Two days after Johnson assumed the presidency, a conversation with the US ambassador to Saigon left him with a very pessimistic view of the Republic of Vietnam's future, without more American help. Johnson told one aide after the meeting, 'They'll think with Kennedy dead we've lost heart. So they'll think we're yellow and don't mean what we say … I'm not going to let Vietnam go the way of China.'

Johnson knew he would have to face an election in 1964 and feared the Republican charge that he was 'soft on communism'. The Cold War still engendered real rivalry with the USSR, despite some lessening of tension after the **Cuban Missile Crisis** in October 1962. The new Soviet strategy seemed to be to avoid direct confrontation, as over Cuba, and use covert action, such as support for 'liberation' movements as in Vietnam. American prestige was at stake. Johnson expressed his dilemma in December 1964 to the columnist, Walter Lippmann: 'This is a commitment I inherited. I don't like it, but how can I pull out?'

Johnson was a prisoner of democracy. He could not make a cool, calculated decision in the circumstances. US public opinion mattered and 'losing to a bunch of Asiatic commies' was not good news any time and particularly not in an election year.

Johnson was also trapped in another sense. He, like everyone else in the State Department and National Security Council, wanted to avoid direct confrontation with the USSR and China. This again reduced the options available. An all-out assault on North Vietnam might bring victory and secure the South, but it might also trigger a third world war, or at least a replay of Korea with Chinese military intervention. In consequence, Johnson and his advisers stumbled and bumbled from one move to another, getting ever more involved, chasing the will-o'-the-wisp of victory through the jungles and swamps of South Vietnam.

Legalising escalation: the Tonkin Gulf Resolution, 1964

The stepping up of US military assistance

The news from South Vietnam in the New Year was increasingly gloomy. All the advice coming to the president pointed to the need to put more pressure on the North and boost the confidence of the regime in the South. In January, the Joint Chiefs of Staff wanted to carry the war to the North, and General Harkins, the head of MAAG (Military Assistance Advisory Group) in South Vietnam, stressed the need to halt the flow of supplies to the Viet Cong down the Ho Chi Minh Trail.

In March, McNamara visited Vietnam and returned convinced of the deteriorating situation. The Viet Cong controlled 30–40 per cent of South Vietnam's territory. Even outside of the areas controlled by the Viet Cong, there was indifference to the government. Desertion from the Army of the Republic of Vietnam (ARVN) was high and morale low. More had to be done. The answer was extra money, additional advisers and the launch of covert operations against the North Vietnamese in the hope of warning them off.

For the USA to attack North Vietnam openly, even through air operations, required Congressional approval and possibly a declaration of war. Johnson was anxious to avoid this in an election year. His advisers came up with the idea of a Congressional declaration legitimising action by the president against specific enemies, notably the Democratic Republic of Vietnam (DRV). The declaration was drafted in the spring, but Johnson was reluctant to put it to Congress without assurances of near-unanimous support. He certainly had no intention of using any such declaration to launch a full-scale war on the DRV. His intentions in 1964 were simply to get past the election in November, without losing South Vietnam on the one hand or getting bogged down in an unpopular replay of the Korean War on the other.

The Gulf of Tonkin incident

South Vietnamese forces had begun raids on North Vietnam's coastline, often planned and directed by the CIA. In this the US Navy gave assistance but not through direct participation. In August 1964, two controversial incidents arose from this in the Gulf of **Tonkin**, off North Vietnam's coast. Two US destroyers were involved in electronic surveillance in support of covert raids when one of these, the USS *Maddox*, was attacked by DRV patrol boats on the night of 2 August. The patrol boats were driven off with damage. Two days later the *Maddox* and another destroyer claimed to have been attacked. Their radars picked up what they interpreted as enemy ships but none were sighted.

The opportunity was too good to miss and widespread outrage at what was portrayed as a flagrant North Vietnamese attack on US ships in international waters led Congress to pass the draft declaration already prepared by the State Department. The House of Representatives passed it with no opponents and the Senate with only two against. The resolution gave Johnson the power to 'take all necessary measures to repel armed attacks against the

Take note

As you read through this section make notes on the ways in which Johnson tried to build up pressure on North Vietnam between 1963 and 1965.

The Tonkin incident

The incident has remained controversial. One reputable US historian, Edwin E. Moise, wrote in 2005: 'The available evidence indicates that no genuine torpedo boats were anywhere near the two destroyers.' On the other hand, Robert Dallek in his biography of Johnson, written in 2004, says: 'Though more than thirty years later no one can state with absolute certainty that an attack occurred, the bulk of the recent evidence suggests it did.'

forces of the United States and to prevent further aggression'. As Johnson famously commented, it was so all-embracing 'it was like Grandma's nightgown – it covered everything'.

The Tonkin Gulf Resolution was later used to cover the vast escalation of the war in 1965. Yet it is wrong to think that this was part of a well-planned strategy of deception. Johnson had no intention in 1964 of massively escalating the war or directly committing US troops. This arose from later circumstances. The resolution was merely designed to threaten North Vietnam and hearten the South. When, in 1968, the tide of opinion was turning against American intervention in Vietnam, which had become massive, details of the Gulf of Tonkin incident were picked over and portrayed as part of some sinister scheme by the president and his advisers.

The resolution helped Johnson maintain his essentially moderate stance, and in November 1964 it was as a moderate who was 'not going to send American boys 9 or 10,000 miles from home to do what Asian boys ought to be doing for themselves' that Johnson won a landslide victory against the Republican, Barry Goldwater. Johnson had appeared sufficiently tough yet not extreme and this worked wonders in the USA. As far as Vietnam was concerned, Johnson simply hoped something would turn up to get him off the hook.

Taking the plunge, 1965

Despite the statements LBJ had made during the election about maintaining the limits on US involvement in Vietnam, circumstances drove the USA into greater action. There was no planned escalation, merely a series of responses to a deteriorating situation. Each move it was hoped would be sufficient to produce stability and force the DRV to the negotiating table. However, each move America made produced a counter-escalation from North Vietnam, where the influence of the more moderate older leaders like Ho Chi Minh was in decline. The DRV was also increasingly receiving help from the USSR and China as the USA stepped up its involvement. America's drive to combat the universal 'communist conspiracy' actually helped to create it. The Soviet Union was increasingly at odds with Mao's China but felt it had to compete for influence in Hanoi by supplying sophisticated weapons such as air defence systems.

The bombing campaign begins

Reluctantly, in late 1964 and early 1965, plans were made for a bombing campaign on North Vietnam to try to halt the rot in the South. Johnson was reluctant to initiate it and sent yet another fact-finding mission under **McGeorge Bundy** to assess if it was really necessary. While he was in South Vietnam, Viet Cong troops attacked the US air base at Pleiku, killing and wounding US personnel and destroying some aircraft. The result was an immediate retaliation by air power. Bundy on his return urged a sustained campaign of bombing as being the only way to force the DRV to the negotiating table. The result was **Operation Rolling Thunder**, which began on 2 March. This was supplemented by **Operation Steel Tiger** against the Ho Chi Minh Trail in Laos. Over the next three years, more bombs were

McGeorge Bundy

(1919–1996)

Influential adviser to both Kennedy and Johnson between 1961 and 1966 as National Security Adviser. He tended to be a 'hawk', favouring the bombing of North Vietnam in early 1965 and escalation in response to Viet Cong attacks on US air bases.

Operation Rolling Thunder

Programme of bombing of North Vietnam authorised by Johnson on 13 February 1965 but not begun until 2 March. It was hedged about with restrictions and designed to slowly increase in intensity. This was against the advice of the Air Staff who favoured an all-out initial assault; the evidence from the Second World War indicated that this was likely to be more effective.

dropped by the US air force than in all the Second World War. Initially the strategy appeared to enjoy widespread public support, with a Gallup Poll reporting 67 per cent of Americans in favour of the USA's war in Vietnam.

Popular it might be; effective it was not. It has been calculated, based on the number of unexploded bombs, that the USA spent $9.60 to do $1 worth of damage. In fact, because many bombs did not explode, the USA effectively provided the Viet Cong and North Vietnam Army with explosives for booby traps. The Ho Chi Minh Trail was not broken, and more and more men and supplies poured down from the North. **Napalm** and **defoliates** were used to little effect. Snake bite was probably as big a hazard on the long journey south as the chance of being hit by an American bomb. Within North Vietnam there were few suitable targets in an essentially rural society. Much of the military hardware came from or through China and bombing near the border or Haiphong Harbour was placed off limits as being too provocative to the communist superpowers of China and the Soviet Union.

> ### Napalm
> Developed in the Second World War and used in Korea (see Chapter 3) it was made from gasoline or kerosene mixed with thickening agents to form a highly inflammable gel, which stuck to objects and the human body and burned with a very hot flame. It was dropped from fighter-bombers in thin-shelled canisters or larger 55 gallon drums. Dropped in this way it could cover a large area and was often more useful against unseen targets covered with foliage than conventional explosive. It inflicted horrific injuries.

> ### Defoliates
> A major problem in countering the Viet Cong was the plant cover. In January 1962, the USA began using herbicides to kill trees and plants in an effort to expose communist guerrilla fighters. The commonest herbicide used was agent orange, so called because of the colour of the drums containing it. 1967 was the peak year for spraying, with 1.5 million acres treated.

The use of US combat troops

If air power could not save the situation then manpower on the ground would be necessary. This marked a new and considerable escalation in US commitment. In March the first combat troops, two marine battalions, were sent in to protect Da Nang air base. The numbers were quickly increased in May. It was only a question of time before they moved from a defensive to an offensive role. **General William Westmoreland** argued that only US action could save the Republic of Vietnam and McNamara agreed in June after yet another trip to Vietnam. There had to be, he decided, either a humiliating pull out or more men, and men who would now take the fight to the Viet Cong. Johnson reluctantly accepted their advice in July and agreed to increase the number of US military personnel to 125,000. He decided, however, not to declare a national emergency and call out the reserves but to drip feed troops from the **draft**. This approach was intended to moderate criticism, though eventually it would fuel it. From July 1965 the USA was officially at war, but an undeclared one.

> ### Operation Steel Tiger
> Programme of bombing begun in April 1965 against targets along the Ho Chi Minh Trail in southern Laos.

> ### Draft
> This was properly called the selective service system. It was a form of military conscription introduced before the Vietnam War to top up the professional army. Local boards drafted young men but there was considerable local variation and numerous exemptions.

> ### General William Westmoreland
> ### (1914–2005)
> Appointed a deputy commander of the Military Assistance Command Vietnam (MACV) in January 1964, he was promoted in June to be commander and remained as such until 1968. He was constantly over-optimistic and tended to underestimate the Viet Cong in numbers and capabilities. He disliked small, village-scale actions and preferred to seek large-scale confrontations, where US fire power could tell. Most of the time the Viet Cong did not oblige him until the Tet Offensive in 1968, which he decisively defeated. He served as chief of staff of the US Army from June 1968 to 1972.

Search and destroy

This was a strategy much favoured by Westmoreland and involved large bodies of US troops descending on an area reputedly held by the Viet Cong. Most of the time the Viet Cong melted away after a brief fight and Westmoreland announced a victory and the area cleared. A body count of Viet Cong dead was usually announced. When US troops left the Viet Cong returned.

The battle at Ia Drang

The first real battle between US forces and the North Vietnam Army took place in the Ia Drang Valley in November 1965. Westmoreland had decided to take the fight to the enemy in an area long controlled by the Viet Cong in the central highlands. This battle applied the tactics of **search and destroy**. The USA would now do what it had urged the ARVN to do and, relying on its superior fire power, simply overwhelm the enemy.

The USA sent in the First Airmobile Cavalry Division equipped with over 400 helicopters. It ran into a major force of the North Vietnam Army, which, under the command of General Nyguyen Chi Thanh, was proposing to launch a major thrust east to the coast. This was a return to conventional warfare in an attempt to smash the ARVN before more US troops arrived. The result was many days of fierce fighting in which US air power and fire power proved effective. The North Vietnam Army lost 3561 killed compared to the loss of 305 Americans. The remnants of the communist forces retreated into the hills on the Cambodian border. Westmoreland saw the battle as a success and argued at odds of 10 to 1 that the insurgents and North Vietnamese would soon be defeated. All he needed was more men and similar ratios of body counts.

Some of the Viet Cong soldiers killed during the 4 December attack on Tan Son Nhut Airbase

What had been achieved by the end of 1967?

Following the losses at Ia Drang, the North Vietnam Army reverted to General Giap's preferred strategy of guerrilla attacks to wear down the superior forces of the USA, and it was not until 1968 that a repeat of Thanh's approach was tried (with similar results).

The USA build-up continued throughout 1966 and 1967, until there were just under half a million US troops in the country by the end of the latter year. Australia sent a brigade and South Korea nearly 50,000. Despite much pressure from the USA on the British prime minister, Harold Wilson, no British forces were deployed. France demanded a neutral South Vietnam and was the most vocal West European critic of American policy. There was growing international condemnation of the air war. There seemed to be little perception that the Americans were the good guys fighting the corner of freedom. Furthermore, although the arrival of General Thieu as president in 1967 promised a more stable and effective South Vietnam, it still appeared as a military dictatorship despite the fact that there were signs of some genuinely effective reforms. The hearts and minds of the South Vietnamese people had not been won. There were periods of fierce fighting in various parts of the country and undoubtedly the South Vietnamese regime had been saved, but at enormous cost both in men and material. Billions of dollars were being poured into the conflict. Could all this effort eventually create a viable democratic South Vietnam?

Johnson was anxious to show signs of progress to silence the slowly growing number of critics. All manner of statistics were produced to show victory was just round the corner: kill ratios; rising enemy desertions; ARVN desertions down; areas under Saigon control up. Yet there were signs that all was not well. Westmoreland continued with the tactics of search and destroy but conflict more often than not was instigated by Viet Cong and North Vietnam Army attacks, and the number of insurgents appeared to be growing not diminishing. Their equipment from the USSR was improving and clearly the Ho Chi Minh Trail had not been cut. To reassure critics in Congress and among the public at large, Johnson had General Westmoreland brought back to the USA in November 1967. He appeared before Congress and on television, stating: 'I am absolutely certain that whereas in 1965 the enemy was winning, today he is certainly losing.' His upbeat assessment was well received in 1967. By February 1968, it seemed a publicity disaster.

Activity: Vietnam timeline

1. Look through the timelines at the start of Chapters 5, 6 and 7 and identify the key points of growing US involvement in South East Asia. What explains each one?
2. a) Plot a graph of the rising number of US personnel deployed in South Vietnam between 1953 and 1968.
   b) Divide the graph into three coloured segments along the horizontal time axis with a different colour for Eisenhower (1953–1960), Kennedy (1961–1963) and Johnson (1963–1968).

Taking it further

To get a feel of how and why US decision makers acted in this period, two easily accessed sources can be consulted:
1. The DVD of the film, *The Fog of War* (2003) referred to in the previous chapter (page 60), based around Robert McNamara's recollections.
2. *25 Year War* by General Bruce Palmer (1984). Palmer was Westmoreland's deputy.

'*The Fog of war*' explains the escalating commitment of US forces in South Vietnam under Johnson.' How far do you agree with this opinion?

Skills Builder 3: Writing introductions and conclusions

When answering questions in Unit 1, students will be expected to write an essay. So far, in Skills Builder 1, you have learned the importance of writing in paragraphs and, in Skills Builder 2, you have learned about the importance of showing a clear argument when answering questions on causation and change.

In this third Skills Builder, we will be looking at the importance of writing introductory and concluding paragraphs.

In your essay you will be answering a specific question. Your answer must be:

◦ Directly relevant to the question.

◦ Supported by relevant historical information.

◦ In the form of an argument which provides a historical analysis of the question.

When writing under examination conditions you should spend approximately 40 minutes on the whole of your essay. During this time you must:

◦ Plan what you are going to write.

◦ Write a separate paragraph for each major point you wish to make.

◦ Check through what you have written.

Therefore, given the time constraints, you should not spend more than 5 minutes writing your introduction.

What should you put in your introduction?

Your introduction should answer the question directly and set out what you plan to cover and discuss in your essay. Your introduction needs to show that you will answer the question in an analytical way – and that you haven't just started writing without thinking. Therefore, it is good to say, very briefly, what you are going to argue in the essay. You can then refer back to your introduction as you write, to make sure that your argument is on track.

We are going to look at an introduction to an answer to the following question:

> (A) How far do you agree that the growing success of the Viet Cong was the decisive factor in persuading the USA to escalate its commitment in South Vietnam in the years 1961–1968?

This question gives one of the commonly quoted reasons for US escalation, and it asks you 'how far' you agree that it was the most important reason. This will require you to assess other reasons why US escalation took place and make judgements about the significance of each reason in bringing it about.

Here is an example of an introduction that you might write:

Clearly the fear that the non-communist state of South Vietnam would collapse in the face of the increasing success of the Viet Cong backed by North Vietnam was a major factor in persuading the governments of both President Johnson and President Kennedy to step up their assistance to South Vietnam. Pessimistic reports repeatedly came back to Washington warning of dire consequences if more was not done to bolster the regime in South Vietnam. However this is not the only factor. Why did it matter if South Vietnam fell to the Communists and/or merged with the North? Here other factors came into play – the domino theory and the fear of both Democratic administrations that they would be accused of losing South East Asia as they had lost China in 1949.

This introduction answers the question directly. It recognises that the decision to escalate commitment had a number of causes. It states some of these causes, and it briefly explains the complexity of causation.

Activity: Spot the mistake

The following introductions have been written in response to Question (A). Each one illustrates a common mistake. Spot them!

Example 1
There were many factors that caused the USA's decision to send more forces to South Vietnam. There had been a steadily growing fear of communism for some time in the USA and there was a widespread view that if communism was not stopped from taking over South Vietnam then it would spread to Thailand, Malaya and throughout the whole of Asia.

Example 2
The Viet cong were adept at subversion. Thousands of government officials loyal to the government in Saigon were assassinated in a deliberate attempt to undermine the regime. This was very clever as, without officials and loyal village chiefs, Saigon would lose control over vast areas of the countryside. This tactic had worked very well against the French.

Example 3
The Viet cong began to enjoy considerable success in the early 1960s, gradually undermining the Saigon regime and gaining control of more and more areas. It seemed only a matter of time before the Viet Cong and their directors in Hanoi were in a position to capture even Saigon. Firstly the USA sent in thousands of advisers during the presidency of John F Kennedy and then ground troops and massive air assaults under Johnson.

Answers

Example 1 – this introduction considers other factors, but ignores the one in the question.

Example 2 – this introduction looks at one part of Viet Cong tactics without answering the question.

Example 3 – this introduction considers only one possible factor and therefore is highly unbalanced and does not show a range of knowledge.

Activity: Write your own paragraph

It is important to link each of your paragraphs to the introduction. So, for Question (A), you could provide evidence in paragraph 2 that explains the importance of Viet Cong success. Then, in Paragraph 3, you could show why the USA believed that keeping South Vietnam independent was important. In subsequent paragraphs you could explain the role played by anti-communism in the USA and the nature of the Cold War. It is important that your essay does not contradict your introduction. If you state in your introduction that the domino theory was the most important factor, then you must maintain this argument throughout your essay.

Introductions: DOs and DON'Ts
- DO look at the question and decide on your line of argument.
- DO make reference to the question in your introduction.
- DO show what you intend to argue.
- DON'T begin your answer by writing a story.
- DON'T spend too long writing your introduction. 5 minutes is enough.

Activity: Write your own introduction

Write an introduction to the following question:

> (B) How far do you agree that Johnson transformed a limited commitment into a full-scale military conflict?

You will need to draw on your knowledge of the changes Johnson made and set these against the existing commitments, assessing if these were limited.

Why are conclusions important?

When you are asked a question in an examination, you are expected to answer it! The concluding paragraph is very important in this process. It should contain the summary of the argument you have made, with your *verdict* on the question.

Like an introduction, the conclusion should not be more than three or four sentences in length, and under examination conditions it should take no more than 5 minutes to write. Here is an example of a conclusion for Question (A):

The success of the Viet Cong certainly produced a considerable shock in the USA and was ultimately the most significant because in many ways it brought together various factors that were pushing the USA to greater commitment of resources to South Vietnam. It provided clear evidence that there was a real communist threat despite the previous assurances that Diem's regime was winning the war. It added to a sense that the whole of South East Asia might fall. Already, in Laos the Pathet Lao were making gains and in Malaya the British had fought a gruelling war against communist guerrillas. The previous Democratic president, Truman, had been accused of losing China through lack of US effort and now both Kennedy and Johnson were afraid that they would be accused of being soft on communism. The charge was particularly dangerous in view of the widespread anti-communist sentiment amongst US voters. If more effort on the part of the USA could save South Vietnam then it was felt by both Kennedy and Johnson that such an effort should be made.

Activity: Write your own conclusion

Using Question (B) above, write a conclusion of not more than four sentences. Try to write it in 5 minutes.

Activity: Write an introduction and conclusion

Here is another example of a question:

> (C) How far do you agree that the main consequence for South East Asia of the defeat of France in Vietnam in 1954 was the USA's decision to become more involved in Vietnam?

Now write an introduction and a conclusion – each in approximately 5 minutes.

Tip – plan the conclusion first. You will always find it easier to write an introduction once you have decided what your conclusion will be. This is because once you know where your answer is going, you can introduce it.

Chapter 8   1968 – the turning point?

Key questions

- How much opposition was there to the Vietnam War within the USA at the beginning of 1968?
- What was the Tet Offensive?
- What were the consequences of the Tet Offensive?
- What was the influence of the Vietnam War on the American presidential election of 1968?

1968 was the year of the most bitter and costly fighting in Vietnam. The USA won its most important military victories and inflicted the most horrendous casualties on the Viet Cong, yet it can be argued that it was the year that the USA lost the war. As the great German military theorist, Clausewitz, stated – war is the continuation of politics by other means. A purely military victory can be useless if it does not serve a political objective. Back home, the American public were shocked by the scale of the fighting after being reassured in late 1967, by no less an authority than four-star General Westmoreland, that victory was in sight. The returning body bags of young Americans, who had died thousands of miles from home in an alien country while fighting for an obscure cause, began to have an effect. The anti-war movement in the USA gained massively from the televised pictures of destruction and mayhem. Even the men at the top began to doubt. McNamara resigned as secretary of defense after months of growing uncertainty and his replacement was no sooner in place than he too turned against further involvement. The president, himself always a reluctant hawk (see page 64), decided that he had had enough and announced that he would not be running for a further term as President.

Timeline

1967	**November:** General Westmoreland gives optimistic briefing to Congress **December:** Approximately 485,600 military personnel in South Vietnam
1968	**20 January:** Attacks on Khe Sanh begin **31 January:** Tet Offensive in Saigon and elsewhere **26 February:** Last communists cleared from Hue **February:** Request for extra 200,000 troops **16 March:** My Lai massacre **31 March:** Johnson announces he will not stand for presidency in 1968 election **May:** 2,169 US ground forces killed in combat; Paris peace talks begin **August:** Democratic Convention in Chicago **November:** Richard Nixon beats Hubert Humphrey to become president **December:** Approximately 537,100 US military personnel in South Vietnam

Growing opposition to the war

There is tendency in retrospect to exaggerate the opposition of the American public to the war in Vietnam. The opponents of the war had the best tunes and grabbed the media attention. Opponents were likely to be more vocal and attention-grabbing than supporters. There can be little doubt that opposition increased even before 1968, but it is important to keep it in

Take note

As you read through this section, make notes in response to the following questions:

1. Why has the impression of mass opposition to the war been given?
2. What percentage of Americans opposed the war and when?
3. Why did opposition increase?

perspective. Prior to that year, fewer than 10 per cent of the American public favoured immediate withdrawal from Vietnam. From 1968 the numbers increased, but even at its most unpopular, there was never more than 25 per cent of Americans favouring such a course of action.

The growth of opposition in 1960s America is a complex phenomenon compounded of many elements. It became tied to the increasing radicalism of the **civil rights movement** and **changes in youth culture**. It was also a response to the evolution of the media; the Vietnam War has been described as the first televised war. Far more than in Korea or the Second World War, the public in their sitting rooms was confronted with some of the realities of war. The destruction of Hue and chaos in Saigon in February 1968 was served up raw, and the image of the shooting of the Viet Cong prisoner, shown on the NBC News on 3 February, was deeply shocking to many. Much of the horror was one-sided. Brutalities, such as the **My Lai massacre**, became well known in the USA and received much more coverage than the mass murder of civilians in Hue by the North Vietnamese Army.

My Lai massacre

The murder of several hundred Vietnamese civilians in March 1968 was carried out largely by a platoon commanded by Lieutenant William Calley. Thereafter there was a cover-up, but charges were eventually filed against Calley in September 1969. He was sentenced to hard labour for life but the sentence was later reduced.

Civil rights movement

Mass movement to end racial discrimination, which emerged during the 1950s from older smaller pressure groups. It enjoyed considerable success with its tactics of peaceful protest under the leadership of Martin Luther King. In the 1960s the movement fragmented and more radical and almost revolutionary groups developed.

Changes in youth culture

This refers to the complex changes in the behaviour and tastes of some young people in the late 1950s and 1960s. There was a growing lack of deference to traditional values and belief in the virtues of 'freedom'. In its most extreme forms it centred on drugs and 'free love'. To its critics, it was often seen to confuse 'freedom' with self-indulgence and a lack of concern for others except if they were at the other side of the world and made no real demands. It was largely a product of growing affluence.

Universities and colleges became centres for much of the opposition. Here, youthful idealism mixed with concerns about the draft were stirred by well-meaning academics and political extremists. The first of the many famous teach-ins took place at the University of Michigan in March 1965. These were a series of lectures, debates and demonstrations. There had been 120 by the end of the year, the biggest at Berkeley, California, with over 20,000 participants. However, for all the publicity these attracted, opposition was a minority position in 1965 and there were many counter-moves: 6000 students at Wisconsin University signed a petition supporting Johnson's policies. Nevertheless, throughout 1966 and 1967, the noise of the protest movement grew, marking an increasingly bitter division in American life.

1965 also witnessed one of the most horrific forms of protest when, in November, Norman Morrison, a Quaker, tried to burn himself. He was holding his daughter as he poured kerosene over his body. The daughter survived, rescued by bystanders. Possibly he was reacting in part to the use of napalm in Vietnam and also copying the Buddhist protests referred to earlier in Chapter 6. It is also possible that he and another self-immolator,

Roger Laporte, who copied Morrison a week later, were reacting to a pro-war crowd who shouted at students burning their draft cards, 'Burn yourselves not your cards.'

In February 1967, critics of the war gained a notable supporter when **Martin Luther King** spoke against it. Demonstrations spread to the cities, embracing more than just students. 200,000 demonstrated in New York and 50,000 in San Francisco in 1967. In October of that year, around 100,000 protested in Washington and a small minority turned to violence, trying to enter a forbidden area and throwing bottles at the police.

Public support for the war

Despite the publicity such scenes gained, it is clear from opinion polls and other evidence that a majority continued to support the war. By a margin of 3 to 1, Americans condemned the demonstrations of 1967 and felt that they assisted the Viet Cong and endangered American soldiers in Vietnam. At the height of the teach-in movement in 1965, 70 per cent in a Gallup Poll said they supported the war, and support was strongest among the 21–30 age group. Johnson and the hawks in the White House could take some comfort from these findings.

The erosion of support in Congress

Perhaps more worrying for the president, was the slow wearing away of support in Congress. Only two senators had voted against the Tonkin Resolution in August 1964, yet by 1967 Johnson's friend, Senator William Fulbright, who had proposed the resolution and was chairman of the Foreign Relations Committee, had turned against White House policy. He organised a series of televised hearings before his committee in early 1966 to mobilise opposition to the war. Cold War expert George Kennan, who had originated the policy of containment, argued that Vietnam was not a vital US interest and it risked jeopardising American interests elsewhere. A retired general and assistant chief of staff, General James M. Gavin, testified that he felt that the war was a misuse of US resources, which could be better employed elsewhere. Such opponents were a far cry from the noisy Trotskyists (supporters of the far left) who dominated the National Coordinating Committee to End the War in Vietnam (NCCEWVN). By 1967, perhaps 12 Senators of both parties openly opposed the war but many more, who supported the president in public, had doubts in private. It was to rally the doubters that Johnson had recalled Westmoreland to testify in November 1967. It seemed to work but the events of January and February 1968 undid any good that it had done.

The Tet Offensive

In January 1968 the military approach of General Thanh again determined the tactics of the Viet Cong and North Vietnam Army (NVA), as it had at Ia Drang in 1965 (see Chapter 7, page 70). Thanh himself had died in July 1967, but the basic idea behind the assault appears to have been his. This change in strategy showed impatience with the slow wearing-down approach

Martin Luther King

(1929–1968)

Martin Luther King enjoyed enormous prestige as one of the most prominent civil rights leaders. In 1967 he threw his support behind the anti-war movement, damaging his relationship with Johnson, who had been very sympathetic to civil rights issues.

Take note

As you read through this section, make a military timeline of the salient events from 20 January to 24 February 1968.

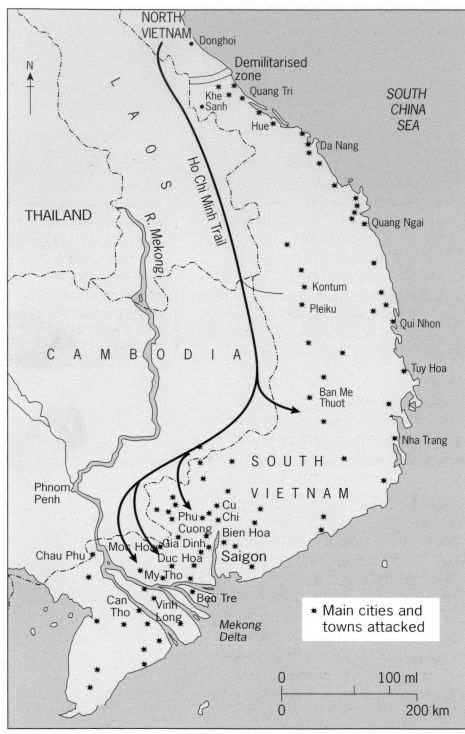

The Tet Offensive, 30 January to 1 February 1968

of 1966 and 1967. It was an attempt to launch a series of widespread assaults on the cities of South Vietnam and stimulate an uprising against the government of General Thieu in the south. It was based on the assumption that Thieu's regime was essentially a sandcastle to be easily washed away by the commitment and determination of the Communists. Planning and preparation was thorough. Miles of secret tunnels were dug, where both fighters and weapons could be hidden. To draw the Americans away from the cities, fighting had been initiated near the western borders in late 1967.

The assault at Khe Sanh

On 20 January a major assault began on a remote US marine base near the Laos border at Khe Sanh. Two NVA divisions totalling 20,000 men were concentrated against 6000 marines who relied on a small airstrip for re-supply. It looked remarkably like a replay of the French defeat at Dien Bien Phu in 1954 (see Chapter 5, page 50). The purpose appears to have been to draw US forces away from the other points of attack and also inflict a major blow to their prestige.

During the night, in the early hours of 21 January, attacks began which were to continue with unabated ferocity for three months. As at Dien Bien Phu, the North Vietnamese had concentrated artillery despite the most inhospitable terrain. Shells now poured down upon the US marines and their one lifeline, the airstrip. It was, survivors recount, similar to what they had read of the worst fighting of the First World War. Marines lived an animal-like existence in trenches and bunkers, their nerves on edge listening for the shrieks and whine of incoming shells or the yells of North Vietnamese infantry pressing home an attack with unbelievable courage. Added to the horror of gnawing rats sinking their teeth into the exposed flesh of sleeping soldiers was all the diverse insect life of the tropics, not least scorpions. Westmoreland was determined not to lose the base and poured supplies and reinforcements in. As a diversion it worked perfectly; or almost perfectly.

The Viet Cong turn on the towns and cities

There were rumours of an attack on Saigon circulating and the US commander in the area acted to pull back some of his troops from the fighting in the western border territory, which had being going on since late 1967. It was a wise precaution. Some **unscheduled attacks**, for whatever reason, began on a few towns to the north on 30 January – they had been scheduled by the NVA for the 31st. Westmoreland ordered all forces in and around Saigon on full alert. Despite this the attackers in the capital achieved some remarkable successes. The most eye-catching and striking in propaganda terms was the assault on the US embassy. The Viet Cong came close to capturing the main building but were eventually all killed. However, the ambassador had to make a hurried departure by helicopter. It was humiliating that the Viet Cong could come so close to success.

The radio station was seized but the electricity was cut off and the taped message from Ho Chi Minh calling for a general rising could not be broadcast. The attack on the presidential palace of General Thieu was beaten off. It was the most protected building in the country. In fact, by the end of 1 February almost all the attacks had been beaten off and their perpetrators killed or captured. Militarily it was a disastrous failure for the Viet Cong.

The exception to the Viet Cong's failures was the seizure of the prestigious city of Hue, the old imperial capital of Vietnam, halfway between Saigon and Hanoi and close to the demilitarised zone. Just outside the city lay the US military headquarters. Two battalions of NVA infantry broke through the ancient citadel walls and captured the old city. The American military HQ on the other side of the river held out until help eventually arrived, but to recapture the citadel would be a formidable task. It took many US lives and many days of street fighting before the Viet Cong flag was pulled down on 24 February. It was a propaganda triumph for the Communist forces, while American families watched footage of carnage and destruction on their televisions – carnage brought about by an enemy thought to be facing defeat at the beginning of the year.

The human costs of the fighting

There were to be two more bursts of Communist aggression in May and again in August. The May attacks were referred to as 'mini-Tet' by the US forces, but it produced the worst week and month for US casualties. Over 562 soldiers were killed between 4 and 11 May, and over 2000 were killed in the month as a whole.

1968 was the worst year of the war for the United States. Nearly half of all US deaths in Vietnam had occurred by the end of December 1968, namely

> ### Unscheduled attacks
> Tet was the lunar New Year and the most important holiday in Vietnam. It had been customary for both sides to observe a truce for 48 hours during the holiday. Attacking then gained considerable surprise but also produced outrage.

14,650. The Viet Cong and NVA had attacked 44 provincial capitals and 64 district capitals. It was amazing and unexpected, but the war seemed far from won. Yet the cost to the Communists was appalling: estimates vary from between 50,000 and 60,000 dead and over 100,000 wounded. Their losses far exceeded those of the South Vietnamese army (ARVN) and the USA combined. The Viet Cong was almost finished as a fighting force and from now on was compelled more and more to rely on NVA troops from the north. But even the NVA had suffered enormous losses. The regime of General Thieu had not collapsed and ARVN forces had often fought well. It looked possible to Westmoreland to capitalise on the situation and finish the job at long last. Unfortunately for him, it did not look like this to many Americans back home.

The significance of the Tet Offensive

The tide of public support turns

The fact that 1968 was a year of military victory in Vietnam was not apparent to watching US civilians or even to some highly placed decision makers. On 3 February, 20 million viewers watched General Nguyen Ngoc Loan, the head of the National Police in South Vietnam, shoot a Viet Cong fighter in cold blood on the street. The fact that the victim had murdered several relatives of policemen over the last two days was not known nor could it undo the impact of the stark visual image. The destruction of the ancient city of Hue amid bitter fighting also seemed hard to justify. The words of one US officer

The shooting of a Viet Cong prisoner in cold blood by the head of the National Police in South Vietnam was watched by a US television audience of 20 million

Take note

As you read through this section, make notes on why the Tet Offensive could be considered a military victory but a political defeat.

fighting in the central highlands were much quoted: 'We had to destroy the village to save it.'

Most damaging of all were the oft-quoted words of the veteran CBS news anchorman, Walter Cronkite: 'What the hell's going on here, I thought we were winning this war?' On his return from Vietnam he called for a negotiated peace, describing the war as a stalemate. Johnson famously commented that if he had lost Walter, he had lost America. Between February and March, Gallup polls indicated that 20 per cent of Americans had switched from support for the war to opposition.

The Johnson administration calls an end

Within the decision-making elite, opinion also changed. This was partly assisted by the request for 206,000 extra troops from the head of the Joint Chiefs of Staff after consultation with Westmoreland. It would necessitate calling out the reserves and the National Guard and cost billions. The request was badly explained and presented. Half the troops were in fact not for service in Vietnam but to replenish the strategic reserve. Reinforcements in Vietnam were not needed to defend a shaky position but to capitalise on success. This was not clearly explained and the new secretary of defense, Clark Clifford, advised Johnson to turn down the request. He now joined the doves in pressing for a negotiated settlement and was backed up by a special session of the committee of the 'wise men', seasoned old hands in defence and foreign policy such as Dean Acheson, who were called from time to time to advise the president.

Johnson himself was rocked by the events of the first three months of 1968. Men who had consistently advised build up and confrontation now advised concession and negotiation. He was exhausted and depressed by the turn of events. His health had not been good and he had been toying for some time with the idea of not running for president in 1968. On 12 March the fairly obscure Democrat, Eugene McCarthy, running on an anti-war platform, gained 42 per cent of the vote in the New Hampshire primary for selecting the Democratic candidate. It was a severe blow to a sitting president; Johnson secured only 49 per cent. Two days later, a more formidable candidate announced himself: Robert Kennedy, brother of the dead president, would also campaign against Johnson on an anti-war platform. There was a strong possibility that Johnson would lose. At the end of the month, Johnson shocked the nation by announcing that he would not be the Democratic candidate in the forthcoming elections. He also stated that he was drastically reducing the bombing of North Vietnam and seeking negotiations. The Tet Offensive had certainly influenced his decision.

Peace negotiations and the 1968 presidential election

It proved difficult to get negotiations with North Vietnam started. Johnson had tried at various times in the past to sound out North Vietnam about a deal but it had always become clear that only the ultimate takeover of South Vietnam was an option. Now even the venue for talks proved difficult.

> **Take note**
>
> List the factors leading to LBJ's decision not to stand for re-election. Which was the most important?

Eventually, after consideration and rejection of various capitals, both sides accepted Paris and talks began in May. Immediately conflict broke out as to the shape of the table around which delegates were to meet and most importantly whether representatives of the National Liberation Front (NLF) on the one hand and General Thieu's Republic of Vietnam government on the other could be represented. Without agreement on this, no deal was possible and for months fruitless wrangling marked the negotiations.

The issue of peace and the war was an important backdrop to the 1968 presidential election campaign, but it was not the only issue. Robert Kennedy was assassinated on 5 June and Johnson's vice president, **Hubert Humphrey**, was selected as the Democratic candidate. He tried to win the dove vote while staying loyal to Johnson. The real 'peaceniks' felt frustrated as one of their heroes had been shot and Eugene McCarthy marginalised. They were reluctant to make do with Humphrey, who was seen as too close to Johnson on Vietnam. The result was an outbreak of violence outside the Democratic convention in Chicago in August.

Richard Nixon, who had stood against John F. Kennedy in 1960, was selected by the Republicans. Despite his reputation as a fervent anti-communist, Nixon had become convinced that the USA had to get out of Vietnam in order to assert her true interests in the world.

Johnson initially tried to remain above the fray. He suspected Humphrey of being too soft and unable to take tough decisions and kept Nixon well briefed on developments. Nevertheless, as the negotiations continued it became clear that the North Vietnamese were prepared to talk seriously. They had been pressured by Moscow, who feared Nixon. They agreed to accept the South Vietnamese delegation, just before the election in November, and Johnson responded with an ending to all bombing of North Vietnam. It seemed that the prospect of peace would boost Humphrey's chances. Nixon was furious, convinced that Johnson was playing politics with the nation's foreign policy. He now played an even more risky political game by encouraging Thieu's government not to play ball and not to attend the talks. Johnson knew of this through secret wiretaps, although the direct links between Thieu and Nixon could not be established. (It was largely done through his campaign manager, John Mitchell, and a leading member of the 'China lobby' acting as go-between.) Johnson was furious, privately accusing Nixon of treason. In the end Johnson and Humphrey decided not to go public, fearing to damage the presidency and embarrassed at the prospect of the revelation of illegal wiretaps. Nixon won the election by a whisker. Vietnam was not the only issue and crime and a sense of the breakdown of traditional society probably played a more important part. Nevertheless, peace in Vietnam would be Richard Nixon's priority.

Hubert Humphrey

(1911–1978)

Humphrey was born in South Dakota and first entered politics as Mayor of Minneapolis in 1945. He was elected senator in 1948 and gained a strong reputation as a liberal, especially on the civil rights issue, which led to his rejection by many conservative Southern Democrats who wanted to punish him for proposing the successful civil rights platform at the 1948 Convention. Refusing to be intimidated, Humphrey stood firm and eventually won the respect of most people, including the Southerners. As vice-president from 1964 under Johnson, and completely loyal to the president, Humphrey alienated many of his supporters because of his steadfast refusal publicly to criticise Johnson's Vietnam War policies. In 1968 he won the Democratic presidential nomination, but was opposed by a substantial minority of Democrats and subsequently lost the election to Richard Nixon.

Activity: Debate and argument

1. Debate the following: 'The defeat of the Tet Offensive by the USA provided a missed opportunity to win the Vietnam War.'

2. Think of the arguments that might be used by Westmoreland in his request for more troops in the early part of the year. Why might it now seem likely that the USA could crush the NLF in South Vietnam? What might also be done to apply pressure on North Vietnam?

3. What arguments could be put to Johnson against agreeing to Westmoreland's request for more troops? Think of the military and political issues at stake.

Taking it further

Undertake a more detailed study of the presidential election of 1968 and how the war in Vietnam impacted on it. Remember that it was far from a majority who opposed the war. Find out more of the views on the war of the principal players in the election:

• Eugene McCarthy
• Robert Kennedy
• Hubert Humphrey
• Richard Nixon.

Chapter 9   Nixon and withdrawal, 1969–1973

Key questions

- Why was Nixon so determined to reduce US involvement in Vietnam?
- What was Nixon's strategy and what problems did he face?
- How was the war conducted and with what success?
- How was peace obtained and on what terms?

Richard Milhous Nixon remains one of the most controversial American presidents of the twentieth century. The nickname 'Tricky Dicky' stuck to him. He was generally perceived as a ruthless self-serving politician. He lacked the charm of Kennedy that fascinated the media but it is doubtful that he was any more 'tricky' or given to deception. In contrast to Kennedy, who had ample funds provided by his father to further his political career, Nixon had had to fight his way up. His intelligence and determination inspired respect but not affection and he was actively disliked by the liberal intelligentsia (those regarded by themselves as the educated and enlightened class). Like Kennedy he was essentially interested in foreign policy and was very well informed about the world and the USA's place in it. He had established his political credentials in the Republican Party as a noted anti-communist in the late 1940s. This was to help him in getting out of the Vietnam quagmire; no one was likely to accuse him of being soft on communists.

Timeline

1968	**November:** Richard Nixon beats Hubert Humphrey to become president-elect **December:** Approximately 537,100 US military personnel in South Vietnam
1969	**April:** US forces peak at 543,000 **September:** Ho Chi Minh dies **November:** Story of My Lai massacre breaks; large anti-war demonstrations across USA **December:** 475,200 military personnel in South Vietnam
1970	**March:** Coup in Laos **May:** US invasion of areas of Cambodia; large anti-war demonstrations; 4 students killed at Kent State University, Ohio **December:** Congress forbids US ground troops in Cambodia, Laos and Thailand; 334,600 military personnel in South Vietnam
1971	**February:** ARVN troops cross into Laos **December:** Australia withdraws last combat troops; 158,120 US military personnel in South Vietnam
1972	**February:** Nixon visits China **March:** Major North Vietnam Army (NVA) offensive repulsed **April:** Heavy bombing of North Vietnam **October:** Kissinger and North Vietnamese agree outline deal; bombing of North Vietnam halted **November:** Nixon re-elected as president **December:** North Vietnamese walk out of Paris talks; Operation Linebacker II – heavy bombing of northern North Vietnam; 24,000 US military personnel in South Vietnam
1973	**January:** Peace talks resume – agreement reached; ceasefire **March:** Withdrawal of US forces

Richard Nixon's televised address to the nation on 4 July 1971 announcing the withdrawal of 100,000 troops from South Vietnam

Nixon's new team and its approach

Richard Nixon chose as his chief assistant a Harvard professor of German Jewish extraction, **Henry Kissinger**. Kissinger became the president's national security adviser in 1969, and in 1973 secretary of state.

Nixon had originally been a supporter of American involvement in Vietnam, as had Kissinger. By 1968, for a variety of reasons, both had decided that the extent of the involvement was a mistake. Both were realists in politics – they believed that US policy should be determined by a rational consideration of American interests and, most importantly, US capabilities. In February 1970, Nixon gave a clear statement of this realism: 'America cannot – and will not – conceive all the plans, design all the programmes, execute all the decisions, and undertake all the defence of the free nations of the world ... Our interests must shape our commitments, rather than the other way round.'

The USA in 1969 was relatively weaker than in 1945 or even 1960, when President Kennedy had famously declared that America 'would pay any price, bear any burden ... to assure the survival and success of liberty'. The USSR had gained strategic parity (equality) in nuclear weapons and delivery systems. Europe and Japan had more than recovered from the Second World War and were now almost the economic equals of the USA. The American public had also lost some of their appetite for being the policeman of the world. The national will for post-war world leadership had weakened and there was a greater interest in domestic issues and a desire to cut defence spending, which had steadily escalated since Kennedy took power.

> **Take note**
>
> 1. List the reasons why Nixon felt under pressure to try to reduce US involvement in Vietnam.
> 2. Note down what had changed in the USA's position in the world since the early 1960s.

> **Henry Kissinger**
>
> **(Born 1923)**
>
> German-Jewish refugee who had emigrated to the USA in 1938 and made a brilliant academic career as a historian of international relations at Harvard University. He believed in '*Realpolitik*', i.e. practical politics based on realities and necessities rather than morality. It is often interpreted as the cold, calculating pursuit of national self-interest, largely devoid of idealism. His role models were the aristocratic statesmen of nineteenth-century Europe.

Reducing the US commitment to South Vietnam was the key to addressing all of these considerations. Vietnam was not seen as meriting the absorption of so many military and financial resources; it was weakening the USA's position in the world. Nixon's desire to be re-elected in 1972 was also an influence, and 'peace with honour' would clearly be popular at home. In other words, Nixon's self-interest as a politician and the interests of the USA dictated peace, if it could be obtained on the right terms.

During the election campaign of 1968, Nixon was asked during an interview if he had a 'secret plan to end the war'. He replied that he did have 'a plan'. In reality, he had no detailed plan, secret or otherwise, but he did have a new approach to the wider international context, which he hoped would help. Nixon appreciated that the **Sino–Soviet split**, which had developed in the 1960s opened new possibilities. He hoped to be able to play the two communist powers off against each other and improve relations with both. He also placed his hope in 'linkage' – in return for concessions by the USA in one area, the Soviet Union would agree to exert pressure on Hanoi to be more reasonable in negotiations with the USA.

Sino–Soviet split

The close relations of China and the USSR during the Korean War had seriously broken down. Mao and Nikita Khrushchev, Stalin's successor, had not got on, and even after Khrushchev's fall in 1964 relations had continued to deteriorate to the point that open armed clashes took place in March 1969 and the Soviet Union massively built up its forces on the Chinese border. China seriously feared a Russian nuclear strike on its nuclear facilities, which was hinted at in *Pravda*, the official Soviet newspaper, in 1969.

Problems in trying to extricate the USA from Vietnam

Nixon's fundamental problem was how to get the North Vietnamese to make concessions. He had two advantages over Johnson but otherwise faced very similar problems. The first and biggest advantage was the serious weakening of the Viet Cong as a result of the Tet Offensives of 1968. This was likely to bring a breathing space for the security of South Vietnam. The other advantage was the possibility of improved relations with the USSR and China, and the pressure they might bring on Hanoi. However, the pressure that Moscow had on the North Vietnamese leadership was limited and its influence tended to be exaggerated by Kissinger and Nixon.

The leaders of the Democratic Republic of Vietnam (DRV) were battle-hardened and deeply distrustful of any deal after what they saw as the betrayal of the Geneva Accords of 1954 – the USA and the South Vietnamese had reneged on the commitment to hold national elections across the whole of Vietnam as a prelude to unification. They were not inclined to make any serious concessions regarding their basic long-term demand for the unity of Vietnam under their leadership. This was unacceptable to Nixon. There was a real difference of opinion between the USA and DRV regarding the status of South Vietnam. The USA had consistently insisted that it was a separate state and that North Vietnam Army (NVA) troops were invaders. To the politburo of North Vietnam, the NVA were liberators who were entitled to be there.

Take note

As you read through this section, create a chart in two columns and itemise the developments that Nixon felt might aid US withdrawal and the chief obstacles.

Much of the hard bargaining between America and the DRV was over whether NVA troops should be allowed to remain in South Vietnam following a ceasefire. Nixon assumed that to allow them to remain would spell the end of a viable South Vietnam. This would be humiliating for the USA and weaken its position in the world. It would also upset a large number of US citizens, who were used to America winning wars, not losing them.

The appearance of defeat had to be concealed effectively; concessions could only be extracted by pressure on the North Vietnamese. However, the growing opposition to the war, both inside Congress and on the streets of America, made it harder to exert pressure. To Nixon and to Hanoi, the US opponents of war were the key allies of Communist North Vietnam. In this sense Nixon saw the anti-war demonstrators as the chief obstacle to peace. It was a paradoxical position. Secrecy was seen by both Nixon and Kissinger as essential; effective diplomacy was not helped by the simplistic responses of the man in the street, whether a radical anti-war demonstrator or a committed patriot determined to see no concessions to the 'commies'.

The conduct of the war, 1969–1973

Troop levels remained high in 1969 and actually peaked in April at 543,000. There was some fierce fighting although the Communists now abandoned the conventional attacks of 1968, reverting to small-scale guerrilla actions. The Viet Cong pursued a deliberate policy of trying to maximise the numbers of US dead, realising that the 'body-bag count' was a powerful propaganda weapon in strengthening the anti-war movement in America. In the first six months of 1969, 8000 members of the US forces were killed.

The morale of US troops was a growing problem in some units. This revealed itself in **fragging** and an escalating drug problem. By 1971, 69 per cent of US troops claimed to have used marijuana, 38 per cent opium and 34 per cent heroin. Morale was lowered by the anti-war movement and the announcement of troop withdrawals. The system of limiting service to a one-year tour of duty reduced the effectiveness and discipline of units, which often failed to develop 'team spirit'.

Changes in US military tactics

Despite the problems, in many ways US military tactics became more effective. The army shifted from large-unit sweeps of the search and destroy approach of 1966–67 to small-unit actions, which increased control of the countryside. By September 1969, 50 per cent of South Vietnam seemed under Saigon's control compared to only 20 per cent a year before. This was, of course, helped by the terrible hammering that the Viet Cong had taken in 1968. It was also assisted by a new secret programme to disrupt the enemy infrastructure, entitled Phoenix Program. It was modelled on what the Viet Cong had been doing since 1960. Headed by William Colby of the CIA, it involved teams of trained US and South Vietnamese commandos capturing, torturing and assassinating suspected Viet Cong leaders and organisers. In 1968–1972 29,000 were captured, of whom 18,000 were 'converted'. In addition 20,000 were killed. It seemed to work and Nixon exclaimed, 'We've

Take note

As you read through the section about the conduct of the war between 1969–1973, make notes on the following:
1. What changes to US military policy were introduced to make the war more acceptable in the USA?
2. What changes were introduced to make the conduct of the war more effective?
3. Why might 1 counter 2?

Fragging

Fragging was the attempted murder of officers by enlisted men. There were 96 reported cases in 1969 and 209 in 1970 – a far greater proportion of a smaller force.

Taking it further

Can the Phoenix Program be effectively defended in a country which claims to believe in freedom and human rights?

Vietnamisation

This meant the progressive substitution of ARVN units for US combat troops. The prime motive was to reduce American casualties.

Withdrawal

(See the figures in the timeline.) The first major withdrawals were announced in the summer of 1969. The last combat unit left Vietnam on 23 August 1972.

Take note

As you read through this section, make notes on how the Nixon administration tried to fight the war more effectively while withdrawing so many combat troops.

got to do more of this.' However, when the US press found out about the Phoenix Program in 1972, there was outrage and it was stopped. It raises issues of how far a liberal democracy can and should go in pursuit of a perceived interest.

Vietnamisation

The core of Nixon's military strategy was **Vietnamisation**, which in reality was a return to the policy of the Kennedy years. It involved the staged withdrawal of US forces and the strengthening of those of South Vietnam. The **withdrawal** was skilfully done with timed announcements to silence critics of the war. How far the forces of the Republic of Vietnam were beefed up is more open to question. Billions of dollars were spent and equipment improved. Some units of the South Vietnam army (ARVN) were very good, but as the scenes filmed of the retreat from the Laos incursion in 1971 show, others were not – there were extensive desertions and scenes of panic. Huge quantities of former US arms were handed over, for instance 12,000 machine guns. The strength of the ARVN rose from 850,000 to 1,000,000. Yet desertion rates remained high, with over 100,000 deserting every year. The problem in part arose from the localised nature of the units, who would often fight well in regions close to their families but desert if posted to a more distant part of the country.

Other aspects of US strategy during the Nixon years

Attempts were made to halt the flow of supplies to the North Vietnam Army (NVA) in the south by blocking the Ho Chi Minh Trail. This involved extensive air operations against both Laos and Cambodia, and the heavy bombing induced considerable suffering in both countries and had only limited effect.

More effective but politically much more risky was the decision Nixon took, against the advice of many of his associates, to cross into Cambodia at the end of April 1970. Although the expressed hope of capturing a major NVA headquarters was not achieved, much was. Huge supplies of stores and munitions were captured and the ability of the NVA to operate in the South was seriously disrupted. However, it stirred up a storm of protests in both Congress and on the streets and campuses back home. Nixon tried to calm things by arguing that it made possible the withdrawal of a further 40,000 US troops, but there were attempts in Congress to block further incursions.

The following year there was an attempt to damage NVA bases in Laos but this time using only ARVN troops. Without US participation the raid was far less effective. It is little wonder that both the army and the administration felt that it was having to fight with one hand tied behind its back.

The reduction of army manpower and the desire to reduce casualties increased the reliance on air power. Thus air and naval personnel actually increased in 1972 to 77,000, by which time army numbers had fallen below this. Many of the increased naval personnel were aboard ships in the South China Seas. There were six aircraft carriers stationed off Vietnam.

In 1972 the NVA launched fresh conventional assaults on South Vietnamese forces in an attempt to seriously weaken Thieu's regime. The USA used massive air strikes to blunt the NVA forces and protect the South. There was a big increase in the number of giant **B52 bombers** stationed in the region and these were used with increasing frequency.

Nixon also took a considerable diplomatic risk when he ordered the mining of Haiphong Harbour in May 1972 to prevent the import of supplies from the USSR. He had already lined up a major summit with the Russians, which he did not want cancelled, let alone a more militant response. His gamble paid off and Russian protests were minimal. The policy of improving relations with the Soviet Union in the hope of greater Soviet flexibility over Vietnam seemed to be working. However, as with all the other military options he used, there were some noisy minority protests in the USA.

Opposition in the USA

Public protests

The pressure was kept on the administration to deliver a deal by continuing protests of all types. One of the most widely supported took place on 15 October 1969 when two million took time off work in over 200 American cities to participate in various peaceful protests. In a sense this merely showed how divided the USA had become; a poll on the day after the protest showed 68 per cent approved of Nixon's handling of the Vietnam situation. Nixon counter-attacked the anti-war movement with his effective **'silent majority' speech** in November. There was also a deliberate attempt to reduce media coverage by arm-twisting editors and television executives. However, the administration's drive to rally the country was not helped by the emergence of the story of the My Lai massacre in November (see Chapter 8, page 76). It appeared the war was not only killing American boys but corrupting them too.

The invasion of Cambodia in April 1970 produced a massive upsurge in protests and a particularly tragic event at Kent State University, Ohio, when the National Guard opened fire on demonstrators and killed four students. This, of course, triggered more demonstrations nationwide. At times, those who opposed the anti-war demonstrators acted violently, ceasing to be the 'silent majority'. Construction workers in New York beat up students and, more peacefully, 100,000 of these 'hard hats' demonstrated their support for the president on 20 May. Apparently a majority of Americans blamed the students at Kent State rather than the National Guard.

Opposition in Congress

It was the growing opposition in Congress that gave the administration more problems. The number of senators and congressmen opposing the war had grown considerably. Democratic senators who had reluctantly backed their own Democratic President Johnson were now happy to openly oppose a Republican president. A series of initiatives gave considerable hope to the North Vietnamese leaders that the United States' will was failing. The

B52 bombers

The Stratofortress was a large, long-range jet bomber designed primarily for dropping nuclear bombs on the USSR. It could carry over 20 tons of conventional bombs. None were based in South Vietnam but flew from either Guam in the Pacific or bases in Thailand. They had dropped over 3 million tons of bombs on Indo-China by August 1973.

Take note

As you read through this section:
1. List the significant forms that protest took.
2. Note down the evidence that Nixon continued to enjoy the support of the majority of Americans.

Nixon's 'silent majority' speech

This speech was delivered by the president to an estimated 80 million viewers on 3 November 1969. It was designed to counter the anti-war movement by appealing to patriotism. Nixon petitioned 'the great silent majority' to back him against the noisy protestors. He wrote the speech himself and considered it the most important of his career.

Pentagon Papers

This was a historical study commissioned by Robert McNamara to show how the USA had become involved in Vietnam, up until 1967. It included classified documents and commentaries by historians. One of the commentators, Dr Daniel Ellsberg, leaked it to the *New York Times* in 1971. It added to the public disquiet about the war and how far politicians could be trusted. Questions were raised in particular about the justification for escalation provided by the incidents in the Gulf of Tonkin.

Draft dodgers

Young men who had avoided the draft illegally, for example by crossing the border into Canada, were liable for prosecution. Whether or not they should be pardoned after 1973 came to be another issue dividing America.

Take note

1. What delayed a ceasefire from being achieved in the years 1969–1972?
2. As you read through this section, make notes on why a ceasefire was signed in January 1973.

Tonkin Gulf Resolution (see Chapter 7, page 67) was repealed, effective from January 1971, and amendments were attached to spending bills forbidding further intervention by ground forces in Laos and Cambodia. In fact, between April and July 1971, Congress voted 17 times on measures to restrict the president's actions in South East Asia. In June, further embarrassment was caused for the president and the anti-war sentiments in Congress strengthened with the publication of the **Pentagon Papers**.

The 1972 presidential elections

Despite both the noisy street protests and the growing Congressional opposition, it appeared that Nixon had done enough to retain support at large in the country. 1972 was an election year. Luckily for Nixon, the Democrats went for a radical candidate, George McGovern, who claimed that he would 'crawl to Hanoi' in the cause of peace. He also favoured an amnesty for **draft dodgers**, a policy Nixon opposed. The result was that Nixon was re-elected by a landslide. He had done enough to reassure the American public that the war was being run down while still retaining a patriotic pride. Nixon was clearly more in tune with the mass of Americans than the anti-war radicals.

Making peace

From August 1969, Kissinger was engaged in secret talks with North Vietnamese diplomats. The first real breakthrough came in May 1971, when the USA made a massive concession that it might not insist on the total withdrawal of North Vietnamese forces from the South. Thereafter the chief obstacle was the North Vietnamese insistence that Thieu stand down as effective ruler of South Vietnam. On one occasion in 1971, the North Vietnamese chief negotiator emphasised the importance of the opposition in the USA by saying to Kissinger, 'I don't know why I am negotiating with you … Senator McGovern and your opposition will force you to give me what I want.'

There was a further breakthrough in 1972 following the failure and defeat of the North Vietnamese offensive and the clear evidence that Nixon would be back for a second term. Essentially, the North Vietnamese decided that they could accept Thieu in power at a ceasefire and a deal was nearly done in late October, although niggling details remained. Thieu felt too many concessions had been made.

The North Vietnamese walked out of the talks on 12 December. To get them back, Nixon launched massive heavy bombing of Hanoi and the north of North Vietnam. Improved relations with the Chinese (Nixon had famously visited Beijing that year) had reduced the risk of Chinese intervention. Operation Linebacker II involved a punishing bombing campaign by B52s. It worked, but the USA lost 15 planes shot down at a cost of $8 million a plane. The DRV representatives returned and made sufficient minor concessions for the USA to force Thieu into acceptance. Agreement was reached on 13 January. The result was a ceasefire on 27 January 1973. The USA had, at least, bought time for South Vietnam and Nixon could claim peace with honour. It is possible that if the USA had accepted NVA forces remaining in South Vietnam in 1969, four years of war might have been avoided – but it remains a 'might.'

Activity: Getting to grips with the peace process

List the factors operating in the peace process under the three headings below:
- US pressure applied to North Vietnam
- Pressure on Nixon to settle
- Obstacles to peace

Taking it further

An interesting study to see how events can be viewed differently is to take Kissinger's account of the negotiations for peace as he presents them in his memoirs (Henry Kissinger, *White House Years*, published 1979) and to compare this with a critical account, of which there are many. For example, see Richard C. Thornton, *The Nixon Kissinger Years: The Shaping of American Foreign Policy*, 2nd edition (2001), pages 195–219. Does Henry Kissinger deserve the praise that he received as a peacemaker?

Chapter 10 Aftermath and assessment, 1973–1975

Key questions
- What happened after 1973?
- What was the immediate cost of the Vietnam War?
- Why did the USA lose in Vietnam?

Fighting by US forces in South East Asia ended in 1973. Already the whole shape of the Cold War, which had provided the context for US policy in Asia, was changing. Nixon had visited Mao in China in 1972 and relations between the two powers steadily improved thereafter. Even tensions between Soviet Russia and the USA were easing with the signing of the Prevention of Nuclear War Agreement in June 1973, by which both powers agreed to increase consultation and to try to avoid situations leading to possible confrontation. South East Asia could return to being a backwater of international relations. Unfortunately, however, the effects of when it had been the eye of the storm remained, and for the people of Cambodia, in particular, the later 1970s were to be the darkest years in their history.

Nobel Peace Prize

Le Duc Tho, the chief negotiator for North Vietnam, and Henry Kissinger were given world recognition and thanks for their work in reaching agreement by being awarded the prestigious and financially lucrative honour of a Nobel Peace Prize. This came from a large fund set up by the Norwegian philanthropist Alfred Nobel, who had invented dynamite in 1867.

Take note

As you read through this section, make notes on the ways in which the events of 1973–1975 contributed to a Communist triumph.

Timeline

1973	**March:** Withdrawal of all US military personnel from South Vietnam completed
	October: Kissinger and Le Duc Tho awarded **Nobel Peace Prize**
1974	**August:** Nixon resigns as president
1975	**March:** Major NVA attack in South Vietnam
	April: Communist forces enter Saigon; Khmer Rouge forces occupy Phnom Penh in Cambodia
	December: Communist Pathet Lao take over Laos
1976	**July:** North and South Vietnam unite to form the Socialist Republic of Vietnam
1978	**December:** Vietnam invades Cambodia and ends rule of Khmer Rouge
1979	**February:** China and Vietnam clash

The Communist triumph

By 1975 it appeared that everything the USA had been struggling to avoid in South East Asia had come to pass.

South Vietnam falls to the Communists

The South Vietnamese regime of General Thieu collapsed in 1975 with North Vietnam Army (NVA) forces entering Saigon in April after a lightning military campaign, which had only begun the previous month. South Vietnam had been weakened by a severe economic crisis, partly a result of world conditions but also a direct result of the departure of US forces. American financial aid to South Vietnam had been scaled down by Congress from the amount promised by Nixon and there was no possibility this time of assistance from US air power. Hundreds of thousands fled, often the most dynamic and creative members of South Vietnamese society. Of those leaving in 1975, 90,000 settled in the USA to the enrichment of that country and the detriment of the new unified Vietnam.

Peace at last came to this suffering patch of Asia and the two halves of Vietnam were formally unified in 1976 as the Socialist Republic of Vietnam. Peace brought some blessings but it was a country which now suffered economically under the deadening hand of communist ideologues. One and a half million people left over the next few years in the most difficult circumstances, rejecting the virtues of communism. Large numbers of these eventually settled in the USA. Nixon enjoyed pointing out that nobody was trying to get into the new Communist Vietnam.

Troubles in Cambodia and Laos

In the two neighbouring countries of Laos and Cambodia the effects of the long struggle between the USA and North Vietnam were also felt. However, the Vietnamese Communists were less murderous than their Cambodian comrades. The Khmer Rouge seized power and occupied Phnom Penh, Cambodia's capital city, in 1975. Their homicidal lunacy over the next three years led to the deaths of between one and two million people.

Also in 1975, the Pathet Lao, who were the Communist Party in Laos and had been struggling for control of their under-populated country for many years, gained full power. They were less brutal and murderous than the Khmer Rouge and closely allied to the government in Hanoi.

Thus, all of the former French Indo-China had become communist. Capitalist Malaya and Thailand remained and enjoyed a burst of economic growth, which brought a new-found prosperity to their citizens. The triumph of the Communists in Vietnam, Laos and Cambodia did not appear to threaten them. In this sense the domino theory appeared false. In fact, the whole idea of a unified 'communist bloc' marching to victory through the world seemed almost like a childish nightmare by the 1980s. Communist China and the Communist Soviet Union were at loggerheads, as were Communist China and Communist Vietnam. Communist Vietnam eventually invaded Communist Cambodia to get rid of the Khmer Rouge. The USA had, in a sense, created the very monster it feared by the extent of power in the early 1950s. As the USA declined as a threat to China in Asia, the communist bloc disintegrated. The age of ideology appeared to be over and good old-fashioned nationalism was back.

The cost of the war

The cost of the war to the peoples of South East Asia was truly appalling. There were up to 3 million dead and as many as 15 million made refugees at one time or another in Vietnam. Hundreds of thousands suffered similarly in Laos and Cambodia. If the death toll brought about by the Khmer Rouge in Cambodia between 1975 and 1978 is considered as part of the cost, then the results are even more shocking. The bombing had less impact than would

Taking it further

Do the events in South East Asia after 1973 undermine or strengthen the case for the USA's opposition to the spread of communism in the area in the previous 20 years?

have been the case in more advanced economies, but years of warfare and instability had held up social progress and economic development.

The human cost to the United States was far greater than had been imagined by any of the politicians and their advisers who advanced into the Vietnam quagmire: 46,000 soldiers died as a result of combat and more than 10,000 died from accident or disease. This was considerably more than in Korea. About 300,000 were wounded and, had it not been for improved medical services and rapid evacuation by helicopter, the death toll would have been much higher.

The financial and economic costs to the USA were equally large and in some ways harder to assess. Estimates vary as to the total bill, but it appears to be around $167 billion. This enormous burden damaged the projected welfare spending of Johnson's 'Great Society' programme and fuelled inflation in the 1970s. In 1971 the dollar left the gold standard (meaning a dollar was no longer pegged to a certain amount of gold). Later the same year it was devalued against other currencies. Ironically, the greatest devaluation was against the currency of Japan, the country whose defeat had brought the USA to prominence in Asia.

The political and social costs of the Vietnam War are far harder to weigh. Initially it weakened the powers of the presidency. Congress was determined to exercise more control over decisions of peace and war and passed the War Powers Act in 1973. This insisted on Congressional approval within 30 days of the president committing troops to action.

The war, which bitterly divided the USA at the time, continues to do so as a topic of historical research. Some on the left of the political spectrum see it as a conspiracy by the 'military–industrial complex' (see Chapter 6, page 61). On the right, the view often held is that the armed forces could and should have won in Vietnam if not handicapped by Congress and a too-tentative approach by politicians. Many simply choose to forget the war as an embarrassing mistake and the only war the USA has ever lost.

Why did the USA lose in Vietnam?

During the Nixon presidency, Henry Kissinger asked himself how a 'fourth-rate power' like North Vietnam could defy the world's number one power. He could not really explain it to himself or others. In reality, Ho Chi Minh had provided the answer back in 1946 in negotiation with a senior French official. He had warned the Frenchman that they would probably kill ten Vietnamese for every French soldier who died, but that eventually it would be the French who would abandon the struggle. This was based on the very simple issue of conflicting wills. The Vietnamese wanted their independence more than the French wanted to reimpose control. The strategy of the protracted struggle worked and the French gave up in 1954. The same strategy was applied to the USA and the regime it backed in South Vietnam.

There is little doubt that the South Vietnamese could not mobilise ordinary people for war as effectively as North Vietnam. Ho Chi Minh's government had the prestige of defeating the unpopular French colonial power. Many of the figures in South Vietnam, whom the Americans backed, were seen as collaborators with the French. Diem's regime alienated many of the South Vietnamese Buddhists by his Roman Catholic bias. Thieu's regime was corrupt and excited little enthusiasm. This is not to say that the regimes of Diem and Thieu were any more repressive than that of Ho Chi Minh. When North Vietnam eventually conquered Saigon, many of its inhabitants would look back on the period of an independent South Vietnam as representing considerably more freedom than existed under the new Socialist Republic. For all the corruption and defects of Thieu's regime, it was far less oppressive and controlling than the regime in the North. In this lay the South's weakness: as Stalin's Russia had shown during the Second World War, socialist totalitarian regimes were good at war.

By going to war in Vietnam, the USA clearly wished to win, or at any rate avoid defeat, and it enjoyed massively more resources than were available to the French. In the end, as the last section makes clear, it was prepared to spend huge amounts in blood and money to achieve victory, but this was not enough. Like the French before them, the governments of the USA and, even more, its people did not want to win as much as the North Vietnamese. Quite rightly, this related to vital interests: Vietnam was ultimately not a vital interest to the USA. Nixon came to recognise this and so did the American people and Congress. It increasingly became a question of prestige, and $168 billion and 46,000 dead was a high price for prestige. The very fact that the USA was a democracy meant that this calculation could be made and acted upon. In North Vietnam there was no democracy and the exchange rate of dead bodies for victory was very different, as it had been with Mao in Korea.

There were of course other factors explaining the outcome. North Vietnam was a primitive economy, incapable of producing the arms necessary to combat the USA. Much military aid came from the People's Republic of China and even more from Soviet Russia. Without this help the struggle could not have continued with the ferocity it did. Also, the USA imposed vital limitations upon itself in order to avoid turning the Vietnam War into a global conflict. It never invaded North Vietnam for fear of a repetition of Korea and the participation of the Chinese. Even the bombing of the North was limited for most of the time and precautions were taken to avoid giving offence to the two big communist powers.

The USA also made a series of military and political mistakes.

- Westmoreland's 'search and destroy' tactics did not work. They looked dramatic – 'Viet Cong' bodies would be piled up and an area pronounced clear – but then US troops would withdraw allowing the Viet Cong to reassert control.

- The small-unit actions of 1969–1971 and the Phoenix Program were much more effective, but already the USA had decided to withdraw and public opinion was outraged at America's adopting the techniques of the Viet Cong.

- The opportunities provided by the great victory following the Tet Offensive were not taken up.

- Even the bombing of North Vietnam was initially half-hearted. Contrary to the advice of the air experts, who urged a dramatic sweeping attack with no holds barred, Operation Rolling Thunder was deliberately launched in slowly escalating phases and there were to be many stops and starts.

- Eventually, owing to the prohibition by Congress, the USA could not counter by air power the final North Vietnamese attacks on the South in 1975.

Whether different tactics used earlier would have produced a different outcome it is impossible to tell. The USA lost; the reasons are many and complex.

Activity: Getting to grips with the peace process

Taking it further

What lessons did the US Army draw from the Vietnam War in terms of:
1. Management of the media?
2. The conduct of future wars, for example the Gulf War of 1991?

One crucial element often overlooked in studies of the Vietnam War is the restraint shown by every president, even when increasing US commitment. Draw up a table for each president and, against each, identify two examples of restraint.

- Eisenhower 1953–1961
- Kennedy 1961–1963
- Johnson 1963–1969
- Nixon 1969–1973

Skills Builder 4: **Extended writing**

So far, in the Skills Builders, you have learned about:

- The importance of writing in paragraphs
- Answering questions on causation and change
- How to write introductions and conclusions.

Now you are going to learn about how to write a full response to an examination question. Remember you will only have 40 minutes for each answer so you need to make the most of your time.

Read the QUESTION PAPER thoroughly

You will have a choice of two questions on this topic, but you only need to answer one. Make sure that you make the right choice. Don't rush. Allow time – a few minutes – to decide which question to answer. You won't have time to change your mind halfway through the exam.

Read YOUR CHOSEN QUESTION thoroughly

Once you have made your choice, examine the question and work out what you are expected to do.

What is the question asking you to do?

There are a number of different types of question you could be asked. Examples are:

- How far?
- How important?
- How extensive?
- To what extent?
- Why?

Make sure that your answer is relevant to the type of question that has been asked.

In the first four question types, you will be expected to assess a range of factors. You will weigh up the importance of each factor you mention in relation to the question. You will need to reach a judgement on the question in hand. For instance:

> (A) 'Nixon's policy of Vietnamisation failed because Congress failed to offer sufficient support.' How far do you agree with this opinion?

In answering this question you will be expected to provide evidence of why the policy of strengthening the forces of the Republic of Vietnam while withdrawing US forces was a failure. You will also be expected to assess the importance of the stated factor – that is, Congress's undercutting the policy – and other factors such as the intrinsic weaknesses of the South Vietnamese regime.

Make sure you cover the whole question

Here is an example:

> (B) How far do you agree that the USA failed to defeat the communists in South Vietnam because of mistaken military tactics and growing opposition in the USA?

In this question you must make sure that you explain both aspects of the question:

- The issue of military tactics such as 'search and destroy' missions.
- The growing peace movement in the USA.

You will also be expected to assess these reasons against other reasons, such as the weaknesses of the South Vietnamese governments and the determination of North Vietnam and the Viet Cong.

Make a plan

Once you are clear about what the question is asking, sketch out what you intend to cover. Write down what you think will be relevant information in the form of a list or a concept map. Then organise your information in a way which best answers the question.

Writing the answer

Make sure that you:

- Write a brief introduction, setting out your argument and what you will be discussing in your answer.
- Write a separate paragraph for each factor/reason you give. In the paragraph, make sure that you make a clear point and support it with specific examples.
- At the end of each paragraph, make a clear link between the point you have made and the question, showing how the point answers the question.

- Avoid just writing descriptions.
- Avoid merely 'telling a story'.
- Write a concluding paragraph which sums up your arguments and provides a clear judgement on the question.

Pace yourself

Success in an examination is based partly on effective time management. If you have approximately 40 minutes to answer a question, make sure that after about 12 or 13 minutes you have written about one-third of your answer. And after 35 minutes you should be thinking about and then writing your conclusion.

If you run short of time, make sure that you can still write a proper concluding paragraph. If necessary, you can save time by cutting short your treatment of the paragraph or paragraphs before, by:

- Writing the first sentence containing your point
- Bullet-pointing your evidence for this point – the information that backs it up
- Writing the last sentence of the paragraph which explains the link between your point and the question.

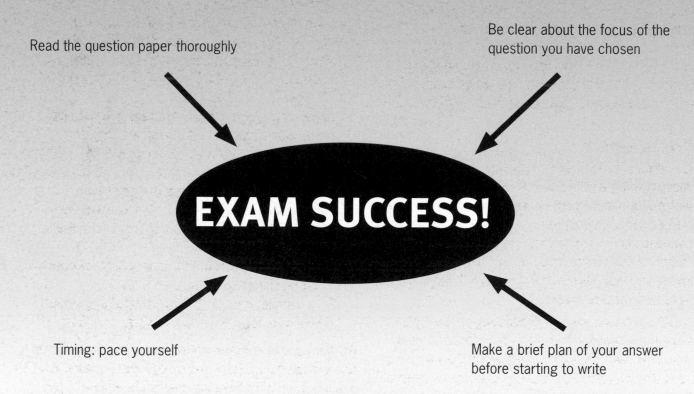

Read the question paper thoroughly

Be clear about the focus of the question you have chosen

EXAM SUCCESS!

Timing: pace yourself

Make a brief plan of your answer before starting to write

Activity: Write your own answer

Now write your own answer to the following question, following the guidance given above.

(C) How far was increasing US involvement in South East Asia in the years 1950–1968 a result of belief in the 'domino theory'?

Examzone

Now that you have finished the course content, you will have to do the last bits of preparation for the exam itself. This advice covers two important elements for exam success: revising the information and using your information well in the examination.

This topic – 'Ideology, Conflict and Retreat: the USA in Asia 1950–73'– is part of Edexcel's Option D: A World Divided: Communism and Democracy in the 20th Century, in Unit 1. The Unit 1 exam will be 1 hour and 20 minutes in length, and is worth 60 marks in total.

In the exam you will be given the choice of two questions on the topic Ideology, Conflict and Retreat. You will be expected to answer one of these and should spend no more than half the examination time answering it. You will also have to answer another question from a different topic. You will be expected to answer the questions you choose in essay form.

What to expect

You will need to remember information, but the exam is mainly testing whether or not you can apply the relevant information in answering a question. You will be assessed on your ability to recall and select historical knowledge and to deploy it (i.e. make use of knowledge to support your points). You can see that it's not just knowing what happened which counts, but understanding how to use what you know.

You will also be assessed on your ability to present historical explanations that show an understanding of history. You should read the question carefully to make sure you answer it in the right way. Sometimes questions will simply begin 'Why'. These are asking you to analyse the causes of an event or development. For the highest marks you will need to show how factors combined to bring about the event.

Most questions will ask you for a judgment. Here are some different types of question stems you may come across in the exam:

1   How far was x responsible for y?
2   To what extent did x change?
3   How far did x depend on y?
4   Did x play a major part in y?

Although judgment questions come in a variety of forms, they are all asking you to balance points. In the case of example 2 below, you will be looking for evidence of change and of continuity in order to reach a judgment about the extent of change.

When you choose your question in the examination, take note of what sort of judgment it asks you to make. The essay questions test a variety of skills. Here are some examples of different skills being tested by the questions.

> The analysis of, and judgment about, the **key features** of a situation.
> For example: *To what extent is it accurate to describe the growing involvement of the USA in Vietnam in the years 1950 to 1963 as 'unplanned'?*

> The analysis of, and judgment about, the extent of **change**.
> For example: *How far do you agree that the extent of the USA's involvement in Vietnam increased dramatically under President Johnson in the years 1963 to 1968?*

> The analysis of **consequences** or **effects**.
> For example: *How accurate is it to say that the effects of the Korean War were largely negative for the USA?*

> The analysis of, and judgment about, the **causes** of a historical event or situation.
> For example: *How far was Communist aggression responsible for a major war in Korea in 1950?*

Another type of question will ask you how far you agree with a statement. This is still a judgment question. You should clarify what the statement is about so that you know what the question expects of you:

> Is it a statement about causation, like this question: *How far do you agree that the growing fear of Communism in the USA explains the US decision to intervene in the Korean War?*

> Or is it about change, like this question: *How far do you agree that Johnson transformed the USA's involvement in Vietnam in the years 1963 to 1968?*

When you are clear about what the question wants from you, you can use what you have learned in the Skills builder sections of this book to produce an answer based on extended writing (an essay) which will help you to gain high marks.

How to revise

Make a revision plan

Before you start revising, make a plan. Otherwise it is easy to waste your precious revision time. It is helpful to look at your exam dates and work backwards to the first date you intend to start revising. Here are some tips on how to create a revision plan:

1 First, fill in the dates of your examinations and then any regular commitments you have. This will help give you a realistic idea of how much time you have to revise.

2 Plan your time carefully, assigning more time to topics you find difficult.

3 Use a revision 'checklist'. Look at what you need to know and try to identify any gaps in your knowledge.

4 Now fill in the timetable with sensible work slots and breaks.

5 Keep to this timetable! Organise yourself well and it will help you to fulfil your potential. If you have not prepared a revision plan yet, it is not too late to start. Put your plan up somewhere visible so you can refer back to it.

Revision tips

- Revise often – try to do a little every day.

- Make sure you have one day a week when you don't do revision or even think about exams – you'll come back to it refreshed.

- Take a 5- or 10-minute break every hour, and do some stretching exercises, go for a short walk or make a drink.

- Talk to your family or a friend about your revision – they may be able to help you. For example, they could test you on key facts.

- Keep bullet points on 'crib cards' highlighting important revision points. For example, you could have a list or a mind map of the reasons why China intervened in the Korean War. Use these for quick revision and for reading during 'dead' times – when you're waiting for a bus, for example.

- Use mnemonics. This is when you take the first letter of a series of words you want to remember and then make a new sentence. A common mnemonic for remembering the order of the points of the compass (North, East, South, and West) is 'Naughty Elephants Squirt Water'. You could use a mnemonic to help you remember the US presidents from this period.

- Some people revise well by listening, so you could try 'talking' your revision and recording it onto an mp3 player if you have one. Listen to the recordings while lying in bed, while travelling in a car or walking to the shops. This also takes the guilt out of being out and about rather than in front of your books!

- Practise your exam techniques. As you revise key topics, plan 5 or 6 points to make about the causes/ consequences/ key features / changes relating to major developments. You could use question stems 1–4 on the previous page, and slot in your own x and y.

- Try doing some timed essays. This will make it easier to write a good essay when it comes to the exam.

- Don't panic. Think about what you can achieve, not what you can't. Positive thinking is important! Remember the examiner will be looking to reward you for what you can do.

Assessment Objectives

To do well in your exam, you need to make sure you meet all the assessment objectives. Below are the assessment objectives you need to meet and some advice on how to make sure you meet them.

Recall, select and deploy historical knowledge
AO1a

In your essay, you must show that you can remember, choose and use historical knowledge.

- Remember – *recollect historical facts from your study of this unit*
- Choose – *select specific facts that are relevant to the essay you are writing*
- Use – *place these facts in your essay in a way that supports your argument*

Understanding of the past
AO1b (i)

You need to show that you understand the period studied. Simply telling the story of what happened will not help you to do this. Instead, you need to:

- Analyse – *break down the topic you are considering into key points*
- Explain – *suggest reasons why these key points provide an answer to the question*
- Reach a judgment – *Decide which of your key points was most important and provide reasons to support this*

As you think about analysis, explanation and judgment, remember to bear in mind the relevant **key concepts** and **relationships**.

Key concepts
AO1b (ii)

When faced with an essay question, consider which of the following key concepts it focuses on:

- Causation – *what made an event happen?*
- Consequence – *what were the results of this event?*
- Continuity – *in what ways did things stay the same?*
- Change – *in what ways were things different?*
- Significance – *why was this important?*

Then ensure that your answer remains focused on this concept.

Relationships
AO1b (iii)

Once you have planned the key points you will make in your essay, consider the following:

- How do these key points link together?
- Which key point was most important? Why?

Once you have considered these issues, arrange your points in an order that reflects the way they link together or the relative importance of each key point.

Level descriptors

Each essay you write in the exam will be given a mark out of 30 and will correspond to a level from 1 to 5, with level 5 being the highest. Here is some information about what the levels mean. Read it carefully and use this information to aim for the top!

Level 1:

- General points about the historical period that are correct but not necessarily focused on the topic raised by the question
- The general points will not be supported by accurate and relevant specific examples.

Answers at this level will be very simplistic, irrelevant or vague.

Level 2:

- A number of general points about the topic of the question
- The general points will be supported by some accurate and relevant examples.

Answers at this level might tell the story or part of the story without addressing the question, or might list the key points without backing them up with specific examples.

Level 3:

- A number of points with some focus on the question
- The points will be supported by accurate material, but some whole paragraphs may be either only partly relevant, lacking in detail or both.

At level 3 answers will attempt to focus on the question and have some strengths (some paragraphs will have point, supporting evidence and linkage back to the question), but answers will also have significant areas of weakness. For example, the focus on the question may drift, the answer may lack specific examples or parts of the essay may simply tell the story.

Level 4:

- A number of points which clearly address the question and show an understanding of the most important factors involved
- The points will be supported by accurate material which will be mostly relevant and detailed
- There will be clear explanation of how the points and specific examples provide an answer to the question.

At level 4 answers will clearly attempt to tackle the question and demonstrate a detailed knowledge of the period studied.

Level 5:

- A number of points which clearly address the question and show a thorough understanding of the most important factors involved
- The points will be supported by accurate material which will be relevant and detailed
- There will be clear explanation of how the points and specific examples provide an answer to the question, as well as an evaluation of the relative importance of the different factors or issues discussed.

Answers that are judged to be level 5 will be thorough and detailed – they will clearly engage with the specific question providing a balanced and carefully reasoned argument that reaches a clear and supported judgment.

Sample answer 1

How far do you agree that the Korean War ended in victory for the USA?

An answer given a mark in Level 5 of the published mark scheme

The Korean War ended with mixed results for the USA. It was certainly not a clear-cut victory as was the defeat of Japan in 1945. The USA had suffered a humiliating reverse at the hands of the Chinese Red Army in early 1951, which was never fully overturned, and the war ended in military stalemate. Nevertheless, most of the original US objectives were achieved and there were positive military and diplomatic consequences of the war, which probably outweighed the negative effects.

EXAMINER COMMENT
A good start with a clear focus on consequences and the issue of victory. It is clear that the answer will examine points for and against the claim of victory and this is rightly being interpreted to include diplomatic as well as military features. There is nothing wrong with the reference to US objectives but a discussion of these must not be allowed to become too extensive so that the response turns into an answer on the causes of the war.

The USA intervened in Korea with ground forces in 1950, with the aim of rescuing South Korea from the invading North Korean Army and preventing the unification of the country under the Communist rule of Kim Il Sung. In this they ultimately succeeded. The North Korean Army was dramatically pushed back beyond its start line by the end of September 1950 and the South Korean capital of Seoul was recaptured. Although Chinese forces briefly recaptured Seoul in the spring of 1951, they too were pushed back and the war eventually ended on roughly the same line that had divided the two Koreas in June 1950. Communist aggression had not paid off and both North Korean and Chinese forces had paid a very high price for their military action, far greater than that paid by the USA's forces.

EXAMINER COMMENT
Precisely selected information supports the student's claims about limited military victory.

However, the USA failed in the bid MacArthur made in October 1950 to capture the whole of Korea and unite it under a non-Communist regime based in Seoul. The attempt to move north of the 38th parallel turned into a serious military defeat when the US and South Korean forces pushed north right to the Chinese border on the Yalu River. The Chinese took them completely by surprise and inflicted a humiliating reverse on the world's strongest power causing a 300-mile retreat, the longest in American history. The Truman government, contrary to the wishes of General MacArthur, the supreme commander in Korea, decided to settle for the original aim of a liberated South Korea and limited its eventual counter-attack to regaining and holding the 38th parallel. The achievements of the under-equipped Chinese troops in forcing the US and South Korean forces back from the northern border indicates that the Korean War was not a victory for the USA. The US casualties far exceeded what was expected in fighting Asian armies that were much more poorly equipped than those of the USA.

EXAMINER COMMENT
Precisely selected information supports the student's point that there were elements of defeat, as well as victory.

However, the Korean War can be considered as a victory for the USA in political and diplomatic ways. It was a positive example of the policy of the 'containment' of Communism which the Truman administration had embraced. Truman wished to signal to both Stalin and Mao that although the USA would not seek direct confrontation, Communist aggression would be countered and this is what happened in Korea. Stalin had re-armed North Korea and clearly under advice from Kim Il Sung expected an easy victory. This was not forthcoming and the Communist powers were given a bitter lesson in the sheer firepower and technological superiority of the USA and its determination to fight if pushed. Mao and even more Peng Dehuai, the Chinese commander, learned firsthand the sheer firepower that the USA commanded and the importance of its air supremacy. Mao reluctantly accepted that holding the 38th parallel was the best that could be hoped for, and confrontation with the USA was to be avoided in future. The Korean War was also a triumph for the United Nations in so far as it showed it could and would fight aggression. This improved its status worldwide, and this was another aspect of victory for the USA, who wished the UN to demonstrate its effectiveness, unlike the old League of Nations. Perhaps most importantly the USA demonstrated to its friends and allies that it could be relied on to fight. This assured its place in the world. It also safeguarded Japan, the most important economy in Asia, and ensured that it was a loyal US ally. Japan benefitted massively from the Korean War and its economic recovery was speeded up. It was, however, a loyal dependant of the USA.

EXAMINER COMMENT

Precisely selected information supports the student's point that there were other aspects to victory besides the military. The point about containment without direct confrontation could have been further developed, in so far as direct confrontation was avoided largely by Truman's sacking of MacArthur.

In one very important way the Korean War had a negative diplomatic effect on the USA's position in Asia. It confirmed the alienation of the new People's Republic of China, and for the next ten years kept China as a bitter enemy of the USA and throughout the 1950s the ally of Soviet Russia. It postponed the reconciliation of China and the USA, which was not brought about until 1972.

EXAMINER COMMENT

This is another example of balance, weighing a negative diplomatic consequence against the positive ones. This could have been further developed by reference to the USA's commitment to Taiwan, which prior to the Korean War the USA had not intended to defend against the People's Republic of China.

In conclusion, it would be simplistic to conclude that the Korean War was a clear-cut victory for the USA. At considerable cost in lives and after the expenditure of billions of dollars, the war ended in stalemate. It was deeply unpopular in the USA by 1952-53 and China had been confirmed as an opponent of the US in Asia for some time. Yet for all this, Communist aggression had been defeated and containment without direct confrontation achieved. Truman had described it as a police action; it was an expensive police action but a successful one: the would-be burglar had been prevented from getting what he wanted. South Korea would continue as an independent state and eventually evolve into a prosperous democracy, very different from the oppressive tyranny of Kim's North Korea.

EXAMINER COMMENT

This response was awarded a mark in Level 5 of the mark scheme [25–30 marks]. The student considers a range of valid points which are well developed. This is a clearly focused essay with much detailed supporting information. It is particularly impressive because it consistently links back to the question. Furthermore, it is well structured as it deals with information in a thematic and coherent way. It is clearly worthy of a solid Level 5 mark (28 marks) in spite of some failures to develop some key points.

Sample answer 2

An answer given a mark in Level 3 of the published mark scheme

The USA went to war in South Korea for a variety of reasons. Some have argued that North Korea's attack on the south was a godsend to the Truman administration, who wanted an excuse to rearm massively so that they could confront Communism. Certainly the USA rushed troops to Pusan to try and hold the Communist forces who were trying to conquer South Korea.

EXAMINER COMMENT

This is not a good introduction. It is answering a different question from the one set. It would be a more appropriate introduction if the question were about why the USA became involved in the Korean War, but that isn't the question.

On 25 June 1950, North Korean forces crossed the 38th parallel into South Korea and rapidly captured Seoul. The South Koreans were driven back to the southern port of Pusan, to which US troops were hurriedly rushed. It was touch and go but the USA and South Koreans just held out. Not only did North Korea fail to conquer all of Korea as they hoped, but the USA got the UN to condemn North Korea and the USA then claimed to be fighting as the United Nations with many other nations helping, notably Britain. It was a victory to deny the Communists victory and a victory to get UN support for the action.

EXAMINER COMMENT

The student has introduced some relevant information here and finally linked it to the question, but there is a clear tendency to want to tell the story of the Korean War. More marks would be gained if these comments were more developed to make the link to the question clearer.

In October came a real victory when General Douglas MacArthur, the allied supreme commander, launched what many thought was a risky move. He landed an Army Corps behind the Communist lines al Inchon, near to Seoul. It was very risky because there were very high tides and any landings can be very difficult, and if the North Koreans had taken notice of the Chinese who warned them about it, it could have turned into a disaster. The North Koreans ignored the Chinese warnings and were caught unprepared and the gamble paid off and MacArthur was now a hero. This was an enormous US victory.

EXAMINER COMMENT

This paragraph continues essentially as a narrative but there are links to the question and the information is accurate.

If the USA and their South Korean allies had simply stopped at the 38th parallel and said that the fighting was over, they would have won a great victory by simply defeating North Korean aggression, but they now decided to go for the jackpot. To be more accurate, MacArthur decided to go for the jackpot and to try to conquer all of North Korea and free it from Communist control. This was called 'roll back' and if he succeeded then it would be a tremendous victory for the USA, United Nations and of course South Korea, whose government was very keen on unifying the whole country. In fact, they would like to have attacked North Korea so in this sense there was not much to choose between the two Koreas - both were dictatorships and treated their people very badly.

EXAMINER COMMENT

The question surfaces briefly but there is a marked tendency in this paragraph to drift from it, particularly towards the end when the question is almost totally forgotten and the candidate presents information as if just remembered rather than information which contributes to the debate and the case being made.

To begin with the invasion of North Korea went very well and the US forces and those of South Korea were able to advance to the Chinese border. This was a victory but then disaster struck. As the USA approached the northern mountains, already covered with snow in the freezing November climate, the Chinese struck and inflicted a terrible defeat on all the allied forces. They were forced to retreat hundreds of miles and the Chinese even captured Seoul. This was clearly not a victory for the USA but a horrible and unexpected defeat. MacArthur wanted to use nuclear weapons and nuke the Chinese properly but this was not allowed by President Truman, who did not want to start the Third World War. MacArthur was dismissed, the Chinese were partially pushed back without using nuclear weapons and Seoul was recaptured, so this was a limited victory but not a sweeping one.

EXAMINER COMMENT

There is still a clear tendency to narrative but the question is not forgotten and this paragraph introduces some element of debate but not in an explicitly analytical way.

Overall, the USA enjoyed more victory than defeat, but it cannot be said that the Korean War was a glorious victory. The war ended in stalemate and became very unpopular in the USA.

EXAMINER COMMENT

This response was awarded a mark in Level 3 of the mark scheme [13–18 marks]. This essay has some positive features as it does contain some detailed supporting information and the issue of victory is constantly referred to with a hint of debate. However, it lacks explanatory links to the question. Additionally, the structure of the essay is essentially that of a narrative. The response also limits itself to the issue of military victory and in this sense is only a partial response. For these reasons, it certainly cannot reach Levels 4 and 5. It meets the criteria for a low Level 3 and was given 14 marks.

Index

Published by Pearson Education Limited, a company incorporated in England and Wales, having its registered office at Edinburgh Gate, Harlow, Essex, CM20 2JE. Registered company number: 872828

Edexcel is a registered trademark of Edexcel Limited

Text © Pearson Education Limited 2009

First published 2009
12 11 10 09
10 9 8 7 6 5 4 3 2 1

British Library Cataloguing in Publication Data
A catalogue record for this book is available from the British Library

ISBN 9781846903076

Project management by the Cambridge Editorial Partnership, www.camedit.com
Edited by Caroline Low
Typeset by Ian Foulis
Original illustrations © Pearson Education 2009
Printed in Great Britain by Henry Ling Ltd., at the Dorset press, Dorchester, Dorset

Acknowledgements
The author and publisher would like to thank the following individuals and organisations for permission to reproduce photographs:
Bettmann pp 70, 85; Corbis/Wally McNamee front cover; Corbis pp 26, 33; epa p 27; Express Syndication/Michael Cummings p 41; Getty Images/Central Press p 48; Hulton Archive/Picture Post p 6; Keystone p 46; National Archives and Records Administration (NARA) p 65; PA Photos/AP p 51; TopFoto/Topham/AP p 80.

The author and publisher would like to thank the following individuals and organisations for permission to reproduce copyrighted material:
Maps on pp 9 and 34 adapted from *Rethinking the Korean War*, Princeton University Press (Stueck, W.) pp 16, 120, 2002 Princeton University Press. Reprinted by permission of Princeton University Press; maps on pp 24 and 29 adapted from *The Korean War 1950–1954*, Longman (Hugh, S. 2001) pp xii, xiii, Pearson Education Limited; map on p 78 from *World's Greatest Twentieth Century Battlefields*, BBC Books (Snow, P. and Snow, D. 2007) p 195, reproduced with permission from The Random House Group Ltd.
p 11, quote from US President Harry S. Truman, 1947, Public Papers of the Presidents, available in book format and from various online sources including the Truman Library's website, http://www.trumanlibrary.org/publicpapers/index.php; p 49 quote from Vice President Richard Nixon, December 1953, Richard Nixon Presidential Library and Museum.

Every effort has been made to contact copyright holders of material reproduced in this book. Any omissions will be rectified in subsequent printings if notice is given to the publishers.

Websites
The websites used in this book were correct and up to date at the time of publication. It is essential for tutors to preview each website before using it in class so as to ensure that the URL is still accurate, relevant and appropriate. We suggest that tutors bookmark useful websites and consider enabling students to access them through the school/college intranet.

Disclaimer
This material has been published on behalf of Edexcel and offers high-quality support for the delivery of Edexcel qualifications. This does not mean that the material is essential to achieve any Edexcel qualification, nor does it mean that it is the only suitable material available to support any Edexcel qualification. Edexcel material will not be used verbatim in setting any Edexcel examination or assessment. Any resource lists produced by Edexcel shall include this and other appropriate resources.

Copies of official specifications for all Edexcel qualifications may be found on the Edexcel website: www.edexcel.com